LB160
Professional communication skills for business studies

The Ope

Resource
Book

# 3

# Producing Influential Documents

This publication forms part of an Open University course LB160 *Professional communication skills for business studies*. Details of this and other Open University courses can be obtained from the Student Registration and Enquiry Service, The Open University, PO Box 197, Milton Keynes MK7 6BJ, United Kingdom: tel. +44 (0)845 300 60 90; email general-enquiries@open.ac.uk

Alternatively, you may visit the Open University website at www.open.ac.uk where you can learn more about the wide range of courses and packs offered at all levels by The Open University.

To purchase a selection of Open University course materials, visit www.ouw.co.uk, or contact Open University Worldwide, Michael Young Building, Walton Hall, Milton Keynes MK7 6AA, United Kingdom for a brochure: tel. +44 (0)1908 858793; fax +44 (0)1908 858787; email ouw-customer-services@open.ac.uk

The Open University

Walton Hall, Milton Keynes

MK7 6AA

First published 2008

Edited and designed by The Open University.

Typeset by Pam Callow, S&P Enterprises (rfod) Limited, Lydbrook, Glos.

Printed in the United Kingdom by Cambrian Printers, Aberystwyth

ISBN 978 0 7492 1789 1

1.1

The paper used in this publication contains pulp sourced from forests independently certified to the Forest Stewardship Council (FSC) principles and criteria. Chain of custody certification allows the pulp from these forests to be tracked to the end use. (see www.fsc-uk.org).

FSC
Mixed Sources
Product group from well-managed forests and other controlled sources

Cert no. TT-COC-2200
www.fsc.org
© 1996 Forest Stewardship Council

# Contents

# Session 1 resources

## Text 1.1

| Report | Essay |
|---|---|
| Written in academic environments **and** workplace environments | Written mainly in academic environments |
| Based on data collected from company documents, surveys, questionnaires, work experience – that is, from original, primary sources | Based on other people's research, theories and analysis – that is, on secondary sources written by academic experts |
| Continuous paragraphs | Divided into separate sections |
| Sections have headings, points may be numbered | Do not contain section headings or numbering |
| Do not contain tables or appendices | Contain tables, charts and appendices |
| May include subjective opinion | Normally extremely objective |
| Very little repetition of information | Information may be repeated in different places in the text |
| Paragraphs tend to be shorter | Paragraphs tend to be longer |
| Do not include recommendations | Often recommend action |
| Include description of methods used | Do not refer to the research method or how the text was created |
| Different writing style in different sections | The same writing style throughout |

## Text 1.2

### Report on the situation with the staff restaurant

| Line no. | Paragraph |
|---|---|
| 1 | [P1] |
| 2 | Because of all the things people were saying about the staff restaurant, the |
| 3 | Managing Director had asked us to look into the situation and give our feedback. |
| 4 | This was about 3 weeks ago. |
| 5 | [P2] |
| 6 | So what we did was we wanted to see what is going on and we wanted to get very |
| 7 | clear about this. So we decided to interview some of the staff, who came from |
| 8 | across the board. And we sent out questionairres asking what people think on the |
| 9 | restaurant. We talked to Mrs P and her team. We also made sure we went and |
| 10 | looked in the restaurant several times. During this time we looked at lots of kitchen |
| 11 | equipments. |
| 12 | [P3] |
| 13 | Everyone goes in to the restaurant at the same time. Which doesn't make sense. |
| 14 | You cannot serve 220 three course meals in that time. Mrs P has only got a small |
| 15 | team. The meals cost £1.40 and the restaurant gets £1750 a week extra. |

16    *[P4]*
17    This is the solution. Have two lunch sitings. You've got to improve the quality of
18    food and have more choice. Get some new kitchen equipment which it cuts the
19    costs. What about a second queaue with a different cash register.
20    *[P5]*
      If you aren't careful you'll lose all the custumers. They could go to the burger bar
      or just bring sandwiches. You can't runs a kitchen like this. The things don't work.
      Everyone is queueing up the same time and that's got to stop. We think people are
      right with their criticisms.

signed: Staff Restaurant W'king Party

# Text 1.3

## Report on the service provided by the staff restaurant

For the attention of: 18<sup>th</sup> November 20XX

A.J. Murchison, Managing Director

### A   TERMS OF REFERENCE

*[P1]* In response to increasing complaints and following the formation of a Staff Restaurant Working Party, the Managing Director requested the Working Party to investigate the nature and quality of the service currently provided by the Staff Restaurant and to make recommendations for improvements. The report was to be submitted by Friday 21<sup>st</sup> November 20XX.

### B   PROCEDURE

*[P2]* In order to ascertain the precise nature of the service provided and to identify the specific areas of complaint the following investigation procedures were adopted:

1    a cross-section of 30 members of staff selected from all grades and departments were interviewed
2    questionnaires were sent to all departments to obtain information on staff attitudes and expectations (see Appendix I)
3    the Staff Restaurant Manageress, Mrs Ivy Patterson, was interviewed
4    the Staff Restaurant personnel were interviewed
5    observations of the Staff Restaurant in action took place on four occasions between 25<sup>th</sup> October and 8<sup>th</sup> November 2006
6    a range of modern kitchen equipment was evaluated (see Appendix II).

## C  FINDINGS

*[P3]*

1  <u>The Current Provision</u>

    (a) staff are currently served at a single sitting between 12.20pm and 1.45pm

    (b) currently some 220 three-course meals are served at a cost to staff of 40p

    (c) the Staff Restaurant personnel currently comprises:
        the Manageress
        4 Cooks
        3 Serving/Cleaning Staff
        1 Cash Register Operator

    (d) the Staff Restaurant is being subsidised at present by approximately £735 per week

2 ...

3 ...

4 ...

## D  CONCLUSIONS

*[P4]* The principal conclusions drawn by the working party were that user criticisms were largely justified, that the current single sitting placed impossible demands upon the Staff Restaurant personnel, that the kitchen equipment currently in use was in urgent need of replacement and that the current single user flow-system was a main cause of delay. Failure to introduce corrective measures would almost certainly result in staff finding alternative lunch provisions.

## E  RECOMMENDATIONS

*[P5]* In order to rectify the unsatisfactory situation summarised in Section D, the Working party recommends that urgent consideration be given to implementing the following measures:

    1  two lunch sittings should be introduced

    2  the quality of food and choice of dishes must be improved

    3  the kitchen should be re-equipped with cost-reducing equipment

    4  a second user queue to a second cash register should be introduced.

Chair, Staff Restaurant Working Party

# Text 1.4

To: Transport ManagerREF: AMC/234

FROM: Transport Supervisor (Field Services)DATE: 6.4.XX

Services Provided by Autocheck Maintanance Company

Ref your phone call about the maintanance of Field vehicles. As I said on the phone, in the past couple of months I've noticed that the standard of service which this company provides has got worse and worse and that this has caused us lots of difficult problems.

Our own maintanance people have done some checks of their own recently and have found that AMC's works have really gone down.

We had two vans doing nothing since five days because the Auto check people didn't come out when we called them though it says in their contract that they'll get here inside 24 hrs. and also twice vans have break down inside of 3 days of Autocheck servicing them.

These are some of the examples of the problems we've been having though before this the work they did on our vehicles was always quite OK.

We've made lots of compleints to the Autocheck Manager about the work Autocheck is doing just now and he's had more then enough chance to tell us why things have got worse but he hasn't replied any of our letters (I've attached copies) and every time one of our reps tries to get in touch with him either persinnaly face to face or in the phone, he's out.

Bearing all these things in mind, you must have a look at the contract with Autocheck as soon as possible and ask the legal dept. about it.

(Source: Doherty, M. et al., 1987, *Write for Business*, Harlow, Longman, pp. 6–7)

# Text 1.5

## Structure of a research-based report

| Key heading | Details of sections |
|---|---|
| Title page | Front page containing a descriptive heading or name, the author's name, position, company name, and so on. |
| | For a student assignment, it probably includes a student ID number, due date for the assignment, name of the tutor or lecturer who requested the report, course number and name. |
| Executive summary or Abstract | Summary of the main contents of the report. It is usually short – from a paragraph to one page in length, depending on the length of the report. |
| | For both workplace and academic reports, it provides a frame of reference to guide readers. It is likely to summarise the problem, the methods and the findings. |
| | For a workplace report, it is often called the Executive Summary and may be read by senior people in the organisation who may not be interested in the details and may not read the rest of the report. |
| | For an academic report, it may be called an Abstract. A tutor may be influenced by the clarity and effectiveness of an abstract as they start to read an assignment. |
| | For a postgraduate academic report, other academic readers will use the abstract to decide whether they want to read the rest of the report. |

| | |
|---|---|
| Table of contents | List of the main sections of the report, indicating the page on which each section begins. |
| Terms of reference or Introduction | Beginning section informing the reader what the report is about. It clarifies the aim and the purpose of the report, significant issues, and any relevant background information. It provides the context. In a workplace situation, this will refer to whoever requested the report, or to any other motivation for the report.<br><br>For an undergraduate academic essay, this is likely to refer to the assignment title and the issues it raises.<br><br>An Introduction may state what the report shows or proves (although it is also possible to save these for the Conclusion of the report). |
| Review of literature | A discussion of important published writings on the subject. It should indicate what well-known researchers on the same subject have written. It should connect the literature to the report by drawing out relevant questions or **hypotheses**. It should indicate whether the report writer agrees with the literature they are reporting on. |
| Method | A description of the research procedures used, why they were chosen, precise details of the numbers of people interviewed, questionnaires sent out and observations made. This should not contain actual information from the research – it focuses on *how*. |
| Measurement criteria | A description of the kind of data collected and how they were analysed. Comments on how reliable or accurate the data are. |
| Results or Findings | Presentation of results obtained from the research. This may be in the form of tables or graphs and be organised under subheadings. Usually, there is a written commentary about the data in the tables or graphs. If the findings cannot be displayed in tables or graphs, there may be a descriptive account. It is important to be clear whether discussion will be carried out as part of this section or whether it will be in a separate Discussion section (see below). |
| Discussion | An analysis and explanation of the findings – supported by examples, evidence, figures and theory. Were findings as expected? May contain a series of headings and subheadings naming pertinent issues arising from the research. May refer to the significance of the findings and may draw conclusions. Or it may just provide a basis for the conclusion(s) and recommendations which follow in later sections.<br><br>For academic reports, it may include a discussion of whether the findings fit with the theories or hypotheses behind the research. |
| Conclusion(s) | Logical deductions drawn from the findings in the previous section. This section often includes an overall answer to the problem; or an overall statement synthesising the strands of information dealt with. It may refer to any underlying theme or mention any questions or issues that remain unresolved. |
| Recommendation(s) | Suggestions in response to the issue(s) or problems dealt with. |
| References | Alphabetical list of all sources referred to in the body of the text at the end of the report. |
| Bibliography | A list of relevant further reading in alphabetical order at the end of the report. |
| Appendices | Additional information (e.g. raw data, calculations, graphs) which would overload the report itself – particularly useful for presenting details of the methods used, or data collected during the research. Placed after the main text of the report. |
| Glossary | Alphabetical list of key terms and/or abbreviations and their definitions. |
| Index | Alphabetical list of topics indicating page number(s) on which each topic can be found. |

(Source: adapted from Manalo, E. et al., 2006, *The Business of Writing*, London, Pearson, p. 23)

# Text 1.6

## My organisation in its environment

*Using concepts, theories and models from Part 3, Topic 1 'Strategy and the organisation' as a framework for your thinking, write a description of your organisation in its environment, and the issues that are important to it at the present time.*

*Specify your work role and indicate how it relates to the purpose of the organisation as exemplified in its stated 'mission' or 'vision'.*

### Introduction

I work for a Charity called Youth Clubs North. The main aim of the charity is to aid young people throughout northern England. This is done primarily through the provision of outdoor education in a residential setting.

The Outdoor Centre, which is called Caxton House Outdoor Centre, is based in Kendal. The Centre has 12 acres of open parkland and lake. This makes it an ideal location to offer young people a taste of the outdoors in a controlled and managed setting.

The residential side of the organisation has developed over the last 14 years. Throughout that time very little strategic management has taken place. The success of the Centre is mainly through word of mouth and providing an excellent product once the clients have arrived.

In order to improve the ways in which Caxton House operates, it is important that an understanding of how it fits within the wider context of the outdoor education industry be sought. This understanding can then be the basis for producing development plans which can be SMART: Specific, Measurable, Achievable, Realistic, Time-related (Drucker, 1999). Through SMART strategic objectives hopefully the organisation can grow and become more efficient and effective at providing an excellent product for its clients.

### The Organisation in the Environment

The organisation works in two distinct environments, internally or the near environment and externally or the future environment. There are two models, which can be utilised to analyse these environments.

The Internal/Near Environment focuses on the factors which can be influenced by the organisation. Porter's Five Forces Model (Figure 1) concentrates on helping the organisation 'establish and maintain competitive advantage' (Tyler, 2004) with Porter's Value Chain (Figure 2) concentrating on the internal operations of the organisation.

Utilising these two models as a framework on which to base the organisation's processes allows the management team a glimpse at what, where and how the organisation operates within its near environment. By basing the organisation on these models, areas of weakness can be identified and a strategic plan can be created to improve those areas of work that need to be concentrated upon.

The external or future environment is a little less specific and takes into consideration those things which are not necessarily in the organisation's control. In order to produce relevant and useful scenarios of the future environment there are several models that can be used.

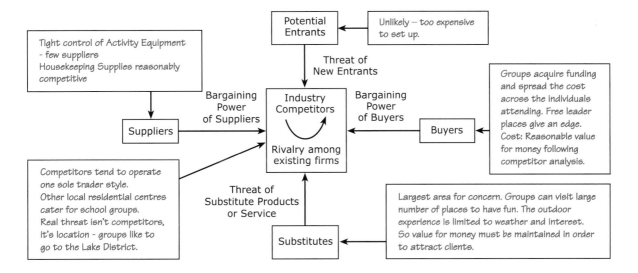

Youth Clubs North position in colour
(Source: The Manager's Good Study Guide)

**Figure 1**   Porter's five forces of competition model

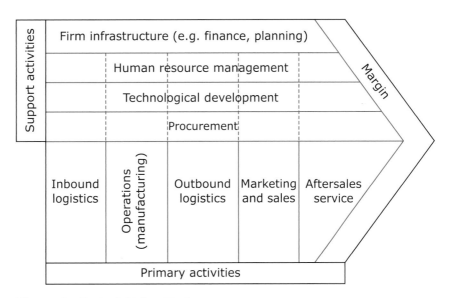

**Figure 2**   Porter's Value Chain

The STEEP model helps to construct long-term forecasts for the organisation in order to produce plans which will give the organisation a continued flow of business.

S   Social

T   Technological

E   Economic

E   Environmental

P   Political

(Source: Tyler, 2004, p. 185)

By determining the possible scenarios within each area, a reasonable estimate of the potential future environment can be determined, e. g. Political – Is there a local or general election due in the next couple of years and who is likely to win based on the current political scene? Answering this question can indicate what sort of policies will be pushed through and on what timescale and, depending on the impact those policies make upon the organisation, may determine the next few years' work.

An alternative to the STEEP is the PEST model. This utilises current and past trends to forecast the future rather than just future predictions.

P   Political

E   Economic

S   Social

T   Technological

An adaptation of PEST is PESTLE which is the same for the first four areas plus:

L   Legal

E   Environmental.

(Source: Tyler, 2004, p. 187)

Again, these areas are used to forecast the future from current and past trends.

The three different models of determining the future are very closely linked and there is in no way a specific model that all organisations should follow as long as the potential factors for the businesses relevant environments are all analysed.

In order to aid in dealing with the complexity of the different models and their outputs a model can be utilised to pull all the different environmental issues together. That model is the SWOT model (Figure 3).

The headings can be directly attributed to the previously mentioned environment models with Porter's value chain dealing with the strengths and weaknesses of the organisation and Porter's five forces and the STEEP, PEST and PESTLE models dealing with the opportunities and threats that the organisation faces.

| Strengths | Weaknesses. |
|---|---|
| Well established business | Set in ways |
| Good facilities | Signs (lack of) |
| Good catchment area | Too accommodating – static product |
| AALA licence | Group feedback |
| Financially secure | Not always professional |
| Recognising weaknesses | Getting run down (buildings) |
| We have a plan | Lack of expertise in certain areas |
| Training (external) | Awareness of centre locally–nationally |
| | Negative attitudes |
| | Appraisals – equipment |
| | Communication |
| | Local labour market |
| | Staff having to multi-task |
| | Staff accommodation |
| **Opportunities** | **Threats.** |
| Funding | LEA centres |
| Rolling MA programme | Growth of industry |
| OPTIC – Outdoor Pursuits Training Instructor Course | Perception of risk |
| | Plan A not working |
| Expanding into adult market | Poor media press |
| Education | |
| Government policies | |
| Conservation and field studies | |

**Figure 3**  SWOT model of Youth Clubs North

Through a systematic approach to the models, and drawing together the information, a reasonably accurate picture can be created of where the organisation fits currently in the market and what it is endeavouring to become in the future.

The Operations Director's Role

My role is to facilitate the development of the operations as per the strategic framework. I also oversee the day-to-day operations of the organisation, ensuring a quality service is being provided to all our clients. This I do through the organisations management team and a standard hierarchal structure (Figure 4 overleaf).

Also with the management team's help my role is to enhance the Strengths, improve the Weaknesses, realise the Opportunities and negate the Threats.

I also have several constraints within which I must work, which are the organisation's Aims and Objectives and Finance.

Aims and Objectives

The main aim of the organisation is to assist young people and therefore all work must be directed at delivering to young people or those associated with delivering services to young people.

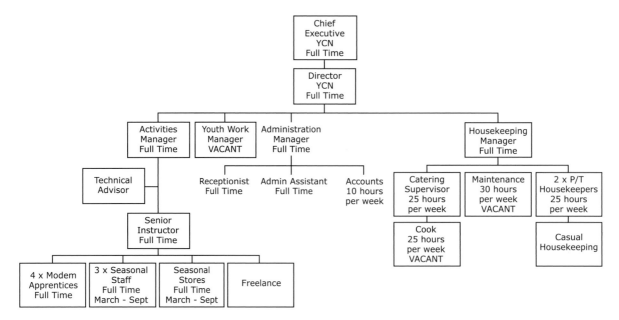

**Figure 4**  Staffing structure of Youth Clubs North

<u>Finance</u>

The organisation is a charity and therefore all monies generated by service provision must be utilised to help further the organisation's aim of helping young people. Within financial terms the most important factor is to break even; because of the charitable status of the organisation, funding can be sought, however funding generally doesn't cover all the costs and can be extremely time consuming so coming in on budget is vital to the organisation's wellbeing and future existence.

Therefore, I have a reasonably wide remit within the organisation and with the aid of a sound strategic overview I am in the position of implementing change and developing the organisation for the existing future. A very exciting prospect!

## References

Drucker, P. F. (1999) *The Practice of Management*, London, Butterworth Heinemann.

Tyler, S. (2004) *The Manager's Good Study Guide* (2nd edition), Milton Keynes, The Open University.

(Source: OU Business School student assignment)

# Extract 1.7

## Consumer decision-making process

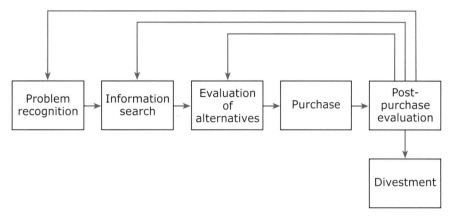

**Figure 1**   Consumer decision-making process (Blythe, 2005, Figure 3.1, p. 45)
(Source: OU Business School student assignment)

# Text 1.8   Mixed-up version

## Buying a 'Grand Days Out' experience

### Introduction

*[Para a]* What would actually influence a new group of customers such as the over-50s group to buy a Grand Days Out experience? This report aims to discuss this from a marketing perspective.

*[Pb]* Consumers are likely to make decisions about what to buy through a process known as the 'consumer decision-making process' which is shown in Figure 1 [see Extract 1.7 above]. Although this may not always be a conscious process in the mind of a customer, it is likely to be followed unconsciously to a greater or lesser extent.

### The consumer decision-making process

*[Pc]* Once the individual has carried out their information search, they will then begin to look at what options are available to them. This will lead them to selecting a 'consideration set' (Blythe, 2005, p. 47). This is the group of solutions that are most likely to fulfil their needs.

*[Pd]* The customer will then decide whether they were happy with their experience or not. This will then feed back into the type of information used the next time they carry out an internal search.

*[Pe]* It is likely that when one of our potential customers has identified a need it is for a day out somewhere that will provide them with entertainment. This may be a day trip or a prolonged visit. Once this need has been identified the next step for the customer would be to embark on _____. This _____ generally falls into one of two categories:

*[Pf]* We should ensure that as staff of Grand Days Out plc we give the customers an opportunity at any time to complain or provide us with feedback from their experiences with us. This way the customer is more likely to become a repeat customer as it gives us a chance to put things right before they go away thinking that we do not care. By putting their problems right it shows that we do care.

*[Pg]* The external search (Blythe, 2005, p. 46) – Here our prospective customer might visit a travel agents, browse through brochures, look at media advertising or discuss the prospective purchase with their family and friends.

*[Ph]* In order to prompt someone into taking action there is a gap highlighted between the actual state (perhaps another bank holiday with nothing to do) and the desired state (perhaps a day out). This then provides the motivation in order for them to take action.

*[Pi]* When they have considered all options available to them they will then make the purchase and participate in their experience with us.

*[Pj]* During the _____ stage of the process the customer will be conscious that they have a need for a particular service or product. The needs of a customer at this stage can be categorized as either utilitarian (concerned with the functional attributes of the product) or hedonic (concerned with the pleasurable or aesthetic aspect of the product) (Blythe, 2005, p. 45). Obviously with the type of service that we are marketing we will be looking to capture the hedonic needs of a customer.

*[Pk]* The stage in the process called _____ 'refers to the way the consumer disposes of the product after use' (Blythe, 2005, p. 47). In the case of Grand Days Out plc our aim would be that they store their memories happily and want to return at the next opportunity.

*[Pl]* The internal search (Blythe, 2005, p. 46) – In this case our prospective customer would be remembering any previous involvement they may have had with leisure attractions.

**Conclusion**

Grand Days Out Ideas Generation Day is about how each and every one of us who work for the company can contribute to the strategic development plans and marketing objective strategy for the next five years. Hopefully, this report offers some insights into how customers make decisions about which products to purchase and will help you think about ways in which we can expand our operations to attract the growing and affluent market segment of older consumers.

(Source: OU Business School student assignment)

# Text 1.9   Original version of Text 1.8

## Buying a 'Grand Days Out' experience

### Introduction

*[P1]* What would actually influence a new group of customers such as the over-50s group to buy a Grand Days Out experience? This report aims to discuss this from a marketing perspective.

*[P2]* Consumers are likely to make decisions about what to buy through a process known as the 'consumer decision making process' which is shown in Figure 1 [see Extract 1.7 above]. Although this may not always be a conscious process in the mind of a customer, it is likely to be followed unconsciously to a greater or lesser extent.

### The consumer decision-making process

*[P3]* During the problem-recognition stage of the process the customer will be conscious that they have a need for a particular service or product. The needs of a customer at this stage can be categorized as either utilitarian (concerned with the functional attributes of the product) or hedonic (concerned with the pleasurable or aesthetic aspect of the product) (Blythe, 2005, p. 45). Obviously with the type of service that we are marketing we will be looking to capture the hedonic needs of a customer.

*[P4]* In order to prompt someone into taking action there is a gap highlighted between the actual state (perhaps another Bank Holiday with nothing to do) and the desired state (perhaps a day out). This then provides the motivation in order for them to take action.

*[P5]* It is likely that when one of our potential customers has identified a need it is for a day out somewhere that will provide them with entertainment. This may be a day trip or a prolonged visit. Once this need has been identified the next step for the customer would be to embark on an information search. This search generally falls into one of two categories:

*[P6]* The internal search (Blythe, 2005, p. 46) – In this case our prospective customer would be remembering any previous involvement they may have had with leisure attractions.

*[P7]* The external search (Blythe, 2005, p. 46) – Here our prospective customer might visit a travel agents, browse through brochures, look at media advertising or discuss the prospective purchase with their family and friends.

*[P8]* Once the individual has carried out their information search they will then begin to look at what options are available to them. This will lead them to selecting a 'consideration set' (Blythe, 2005, p. 47). This is the group of solutions that are most likely to fulfil their needs.

*[P9]* When they have considered all options available to them they will then make the purchase and participate in their experience with us.

*[P10]* The customer will then decide whether they were happy with their experience or not. This will then feed back into the type of information used previously for their internal search for next time.

*[P11]* The stage in the process called divestment 'refers to the way the consumer disposes of the product after use' (Blythe, 2005, p. 47). In the case of Grand Days Out plc our aim would be that they store their memories happily and want to return at the next opportunity.

*[P12]* We should ensure that as staff of Grand Days Out plc we give the customers an opportunity at any time to complain or provide us with feedback from their experiences with us. This way the customer is more likely to become a repeat customer as it gives us a chance to put things right before they go away thinking that we do not care. By putting their problems right it shows that we do care.

**Conclusion**

Grand Days Out Ideas Generation Day is about how each and every one of us who work for the company can contribute to the strategic development plans and marketing objective strategy for the next five years. Hopefully, this report offers some insights into how customers make decisions about which products to purchase and will help you think about ways in which we can expand our operations to attract the growing and affluent market segment of older consumers.

(Source: OU Business School student assignment)

# Text 1.10

## UK equity market – thank heavens!

Does God exist? Attempting to answer such a daunting question might appear to be somewhat beyond the normal scope of a humble 'two-sider' broking report, but circumstances force one to seriously consider the issue. Flying almost invariably does. Being able, from 24,000 feet, to phone our New York office to ascertain the result of the Maastricht vote is certainly a miracle of modern technology and pushes one towards a positive conclusion. The clincher, of course, is the result itself; a positive vote for Major, the Government, Europe, the economy and, last but by no means least, the stock market. The vote may have been close but we doubt it really matters – common sense prevailed and Major won, that's all that counts – remember our recent title 'Never Mind the Politics, Feel the Policy', we stand 100% behind the trust of this statement. Heaven, for the bull, can wait; what lies ahead in the UK stock market is too good to miss.

(Extract from an equity analyst flyer, 1992)

# Text 1.11

## The Netherlands

After peaking at 4.4% in April 2000, inflation fell steadily during the second half of last year, helped in part by lower oil prices and a 1% cut in VAT in October. Inflation declined to 2.4% in February and was 1.8% below that in Germany which represents the best relative performance since mid-1998. The outlook for inflation seems reasonable in 1993. Wage claims are in a range of 3–3.5%, down about one percentage point on last year's outturn. Service sector inflation remains stubbornly high but is likely to improve in response to the weakness of the economy. Our forecasts show inflation subsiding from 3.6% in 2000 to 2.3% this year and to 1.9% in 2002. Partly in response to these favourable inflation developments ...

(Extract from Goldman Sachs economic forecast, 1992)

# Text 1.12

## Time frames and verb forms (with gaps)

| PAST | PRESENT | FUTURE |
|---|---|---|
| It _____ originally a family company | | We _____ to a new factory next year |
| It _____ only one product | | We _____ to expand |
| It _____ in 1902 | | We _____ a sales campaign soon |
| It _____ by two brothers who _____ as engineers | | |
| They _____ some market research before they set up the company | | |
| It _____ several successful acquisitions since 1958 | | |
| It _____ the turbine market for years | | |
| It _____ plastics since 1958 | | |
| It _____ recently _____ the soft drinks field | It now _____ in several countries | |
| | It _____ rapidly | |

| 1900 | 1902 | 1958 | 2000 | 2008– |
|---|---|---|---|---|

# Text 1.13

## Time frames and verb forms

| PAST | | PRESENT | FUTURE |
|---|---|---|---|
| | | | We **are moving** to a new factory next year |
| | | | We **will continue** to expand |
| | | | We **are going to launch** a sales campaign soon |
| | It **has made** several successful acquisitions since 1958 | | |
| | It **has led** the turbine market for years | | |
| | | It now **operates** in several countries | |
| | It **has been producing** plastics since 1958 | It **is expanding** rapidly | |
| It **was** originally a family company | | | |
| It **had** only one product | | | |
| It **started** in 1902 | | | |
| It **was founded** by two brothers who **were working** as engineers | | | |
| | It **has** recently **entered** the soft drinks field | | |
| They **had done** some market research before they set up the company | | | |
| 1900 | 1902 | 1958 | 2000 | 2008– |

(Source: adapted from Brieger, N. and Comfort, J., 1992, *Language Reference for Business English*, London, Prentice-Hall, p. 25)

# Session 2 resources

## Text 2.1

### CONTENTS

|  | **PAGES** |
|---|---|
| TASK 1 | 1 – 9 |
| TASK 2 | 10 – 17 |
| TASK 3 | 18 – 22 |
| TASK 4 | 23 – 30 |
| REFERENCES | |

### TASK 1

*Using the concepts, theories and models from Part 3, Topic 1 'Strategy and the organisation' as a framework for your thinking, write a description of your organisation in its environment, and the issues that are important to it at the present time.*

*Specify your work role and indicate how it relates to the purpose of the organisation as exemplified in its stated 'mission' or 'vision'.*

### BACKGROUND

Thrift Bank began as a tiny Belfast banking company called the Thrift Banking Partnership. From the very beginning, Thrift catered to the business market and expanded services in line with this need.

Throughout its history, the bank's fortunes have been closely linked with the border counties and Dublin. In 1840, the Bank established its first branch in what is now the Republic of Ireland and significantly expanded the branch network during the 1970s. Following a take-over in the late eighties, these outlets were renamed National Thrift Bank.

Today, Thrift remains the bank of choice for the majority of businesses in Northern Ireland. There are 95 Branches and 11 Business Centres. A world-wide network of sister banks provides business customers with on-the-spot banking and financial assistance in countries where they wish to conduct business.

Thrift has now been bought out by a Dutch company called 'Utrecht Bank'. The changeover to the new ownership will occur on 18 April 2006.

The exchange relationship diagram (Figure 1) helps to explain the management within the Thrift Bank and my work role (indicated in the coloured box).

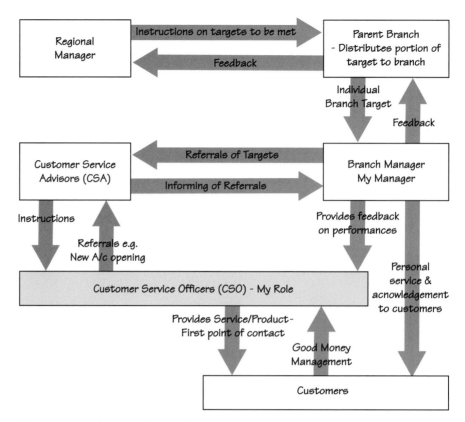

**Figure 1**   Exchange relationship

## WORK ROLES

- There are four Regional Managers throughout Northern Ireland - North Region (22 Branches), South & West Region (24 Branches), Belfast Region (25 Branches) and East Region (24 Branches). Altogether a total of 95 branches.

- The Regional Manager gives instructions on targets to be met to the Parent Branch Manager.

- The Parent Branch Manager then distributes portions of the target to be met to individual branches.

- The Branch Manager makes referrals of the targets to the Customer Service Advisers.

- The Customer Service Advisers give instructions and guidance to the Customer Service Officers in order for the Customer Service Officers to provide services/products.

- **The Customer Service Officer makes referrals to the Customer Service Advisers, who then forward the referrals to the Branch Manager.**

- **Customer Service Officers are first point of contact, and provide customers with products/service.**

(The above two points highlighted give a brief description of my work role.)

## DESCRIPTION OF MY ORGANISATION

I have chosen 'Porter's five forces model' to describe my organisation. I think it suits my employment in an established competitive financial business as 'Porter identifies five types of competitive pressure within a sector: established competitors, new entrants to the market, substitute products, the bargaining power of suppliers and that of customers'.

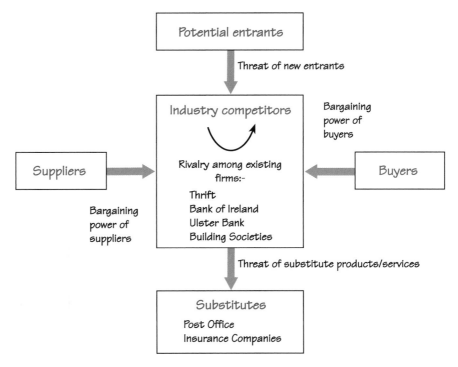

**Figure 2**  Porter's five forces model of competition (Source: Porter, 1980)

Above I have used Porter's five forces model (Figure 2) to display the competition which my organisation faces.

Being a new member of staff in a financial sector allows me to identify with all of the above five types. In the town in which I work there are 5 different Building Societies and 2 other established competitors (Bank of Ireland and Ulster Bank) which are all seen as a threat to our service. As mentioned previously 'Thrift' has been bought out by a Dutch company called 'Utrecht Bank'. In Holland, Utrecht Bank is an old, distinguished and select bank – a market leader and a strong commercial bank that also attracts affluent retail customers. The changeover will occur at Easter 2006 and will involve all employees going on new training and slight changes occurring to our logo (but not many, as Thrift does not want people to think it is a different business altogether).  This type of banking will be a threat to other financial providers throughout Northern Ireland.

Porter argues that rivalry among existing firms is not the only competitive force but the availability of substitutes, the strength of suppliers and buyers (customers) and the threat of new entrants. From the model used you can see that I have chosen the Post Office and Insurance Companies as substitutes.  The reason is that these substitutes <u>can</u> offer cheaper exchange bureau (currency), better interest rates on savings, cheaper mortgage rates, house insurance, etc. Substitutes like the examples I have given can take a large chunk of financial business away from our everyday service as the attraction of 'more for your money' goes a long way.

Porter explains that suppliers are important as their relative power can determine what proportion of the price of the final product they capture. For example the competitors put pressure on the suppliers to reduce their prices and thus their profit margins too. This is why brand recognition is important when entering a market as there are various levels of barriers to gain entry, requiring heavy capital investment by new entrants.

To summarise, the model clearly displays where my firm and its competitors are at present. It is a clear way of identifying what competition is in place and makes my understanding of why my role as a customer service officer is so important, as I am first point of contact.

## THE PURPOSE OF MY ORGANISATION'S 'MISSION' OR 'VISION' STATEMENT

The evidence that my organisation has a 'good' mission statement is as follows.

---

**Thrift Bank – Mission Statement**

*Our Vision*

To be the world's leading financial services company

*Our Mission*

We tailor financial services to help individuals, families, businesses and communities to achieve their goals

*Our Values*

– Service to our customers

– Quality in everything we do

– Professionalism and ethics in all our actions

– Competitiveness and a will to win

– Growth and development of our people

– Continuous productivity improvement

– Growing profit for our stakeholders

---

- The mission statement clearly shows what the organisation wants to be and is concise and to the point 'We tailor financial services to help individuals, families, businesses and communities to achieve their goals'.
- It shows the organisation's purpose for existing 'To be the world's leading financial services company'.
- It contains the organisation's key values:
    Service to our customers
    Quality in everything we do
    Professionalism and ethics in all our actions
    Competitiveness and a will to win
    Growth and development of our people
    Continuous productivity improvement
    Growing profit for our stakeholders.

- In my opinion my organisation meets the criteria of 'The six F test' of *The Manager's Good Study Guide*:

1  Fantastic – It draws your attention with its unique colour 'blue' (not shown on mission statement).

2  Feasible – As a new employee, I am learning that this area is definitely included. Everyone works well as a team and puts in overtime to achieve our goals.

3  Focused – I know that our organisation was bought out by a 'Dutch' company and changes will be made in April 06. In order for this project to be completed a number of new staff were employed to fulfil the requirements of the project. This meant that new training would need to take place along with many other changes in order to have a successful outcome.

4  Flexible – Because Thrift is the largest financial retail bank in Northern Ireland, it has already shown that there is plenty of room for manoeuvre.

5  Faxable – I think the vision statement 'To be the world's leading financial services company' could prove to be remembered easily.

6  Fun – It's fun because it caters for all, individuals, families, businesses and communities.

CONCLUSION

The 'Exchange Relationship' diagram shows the relationship between my role and the customer. As I am first point of contact, my role as a 'Customer Service Officer' gives a first impression to the customer.

'Description of my workplace' describes the competition between Thrift and other financial providers, which leads on to how important our changeover will be when it occurs in April 06. This also means that our existing 'mission' or 'vision' statement will change for the best with the hope that Thrift to become a leading financial provider again!

(Source: OU Business School student assignment)

# Text 2.2

## My organisation in its environment

*Using concepts, theories and models from Part 3, Topic 1 'Strategy and the organisation' as a framework for your thinking, write a description of your organisation in its environment, and the issues that are important to it at the present time.*

*Specify your work role and indicate how it relates to the purpose of the organisation as exemplified in its stated 'mission' or 'vision'.*

Introduction

I work for a Charity called Youth Clubs North. The main aim of the charity is to aid young people throughout northern England. This is done primarily through the provision of outdoor education in a residential setting.

The Outdoor Centre, which is called Caxton House Outdoor Centre, is based in Kendal. The Centre has 12 acres of open parkland and lake. This makes it an ideal location to offer young people a taste of the outdoors in a controlled and managed setting.

The residential side of the organisation has developed over the last 14 years. Throughout that time very little strategic management has taken place. The success of the Centre is mainly through word of mouth and providing an excellent product once the clients have arrived.

In order to improve the ways in which Caxton House operates, it is important that an understanding of how it fits within the wider context of the outdoor education industry be sought. This understanding can then be the basis for producing development plans which can be SMART: Specific, Measurable, Achievable, Realistic, Time-related (Drucker, 1999). Through SMART strategic objectives hopefully the organisation can grow and become more efficient and effective at providing an excellent product for its clients.

The Organisation in the Environment

The organisation works in two distinct environments, internally or the near environment and externally or the future environment. There are two models, which can be utilised to analyse these environments.

The Internal/Near Environment focuses on the factors which can be influenced by the organisation. Porter's Five Forces Model (Figure 1) concentrates on helping the organisation 'establish and maintain competitive advantage' (Tyler, 2004) with Porter's Value Chain (Figure 2) concentrating on the internal operations of the organisation.

Utilising these two models as a framework on which to base the organisation's processes allows the management team a glimpse at what, where and how the organisation operates within its near environment. By basing the organisation on these models, areas of weakness can be identified and a strategic plan can be created to improve those areas of work that need to be concentrated upon.

The external or future environment is a little less specific and takes into consideration those things which are not necessarily in the organisation's control. In order to produce relevant and useful scenarios of the future environment there are several models that can be used.

The STEEP model helps to construct long-term forecasts for the organisation in order to produce plans which will give the organisation a continued flow of business.

S   Social
T   Technological
E   Economic
E   Environmental
P   Political

(Source: Tyler, 2004, p. 185)

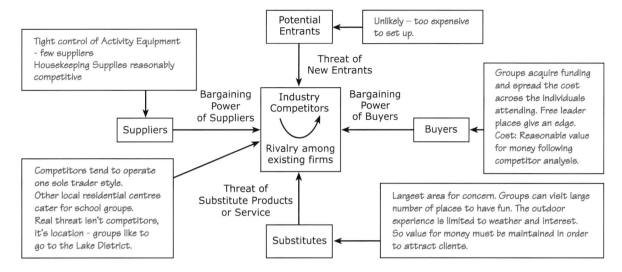

Youth Clubs North position in colour
(Source: The Manager's Good Study Guide)

**Figure 1**   Porter's five forces of competition model

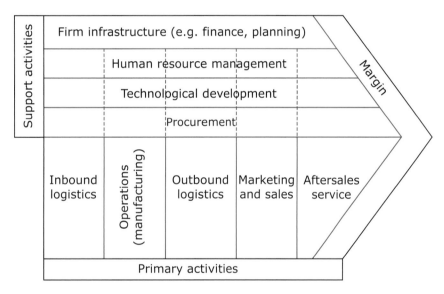

**Figure 2**   Porter's Value Chain

By determining the possible scenarios within each area, a reasonable estimate of the potential future environment can be determined, e.g. Political – Is there a local or general election due in the next couple of years and who is likely to win based on the current political scene? Answering this question can indicate what sort of policies will be pushed through and on what timescale and, depending on the impact those policies make upon the organisation, may determine the next few years' work.

An alternative to the STEEP is the PEST model. This utilises current and past trends to forecast the future rather than just future predictions.

    P    Political

    E    Economic

    S    Social

    T    Technological

An adaptation of PEST is PESTLE which is the same for the first four areas plus:

L   Legal

E   Environmental.

(Source: Tyler, 2004, p. 187)

Again, these areas are used to forecast the future from current and past trends.

The three different models of determining the future are very closely linked and there is in no way a specific model that all organisations should follow as long as the potential factors for the businesses relevant environments are all analysed.

In order to aid in dealing with the complexity of the different models and their outputs a model can be utilised to pull all the different environmental issues together. That model is the SWOT model (Figure 3).

| Strengths | Weaknesses |
|---|---|
| Well established business | Set in ways |
| Good facilities | Signs (lack of) |
| Good catchment area | Too accommodating – static product |
| AALA licence | Group feedback |
| Financially secure | Not always professional |
| Recognising weaknesses | Getting run down (buildings) |
| We have a plan | Lack of expertise in certain areas |
| Training (external) | Awareness of centre locally–nationally |
| | Negative attitudes |
| | Appraisals – equipment |
| | Communication |
| | Local labour market |
| | Staff having to multi-task |
| | Staff accommodation |
| **Opportunities** | **Threats** |
| Funding | LEA centres |
| Rolling MA programme | Growth of industry |
| OPTIC – Outdoor Pursuits Training Instructor Course | Perception of risk |
| Expanding into adult market | Plan A not working |
| Education | Poor media press |
| Government policies | |
| Conservation and field studies | |

**Figure 3**   SWOT model of Youth Clubs North

The headings can be directly attributed to the previously mentioned environment models with Porter's value chain dealing with the strengths and weaknesses of the organisation and Porter's five forces and the STEEP, PEST and PESTLE models dealing with the opportunities and threats that the organisation faces.

Through a systematic approach to the models, and drawing together the information, a reasonably accurate picture can be created of where the organisation fits currently in the market and what it is endeavouring to become in the future.

<u>The Operations Director's Role</u>

My role is to facilitate the development of the operations as per the strategic framework. I also oversee the day-to-day operations of the organisation, ensuring a quality service is being provided to all our clients. This I do through the organisations management team and a standard hierarchal structure (Figure 4).

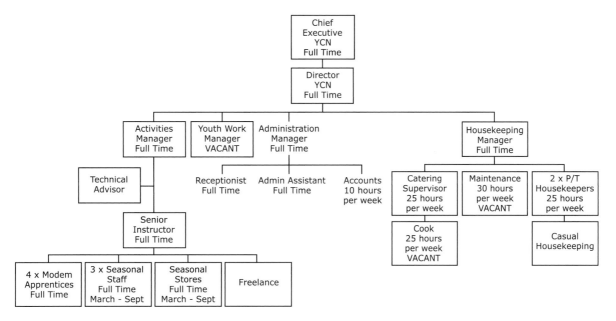

**Figure 4**   Staffing structure of Youth Clubs North

Also with the management team's help my role is to enhance the Strengths, improve the Weaknesses, realise the Opportunities and negate the Threats.

I also have several constraints within which I must work, which are the organisation's Aims and Objectives and Finance.

<u>Aims and Objectives</u>

The main aim of the organisation is to assist young people and therefore all work must be directed at delivering to young people or those associated with delivering services to young people.

<u>Finance</u>

The organisation is a charity and therefore all monies generated by service provision must be utilised to help further the organisation's aim of helping young people. Within financial terms the most important factor is to break even; because of the charitable status of the organisation, funding can be sought, however funding generally doesn't cover all the costs and can be extremely time consuming so coming in on budget is vital to the organisation's wellbeing and future existence.

Therefore, I have a reasonably wide remit within the organisation and with the aid of a sound strategic overview I am in the position of implementing change and developing the organisation for the existing future. A very exciting prospect!

## References

Drucker, P. F. (1999) *The Practice of Management*, London, Butterworth Heinemann.

Tyler, S. (2004) *The Manager's Good Study Guide* (2nd edition), Milton Keynes, The Open University.

(Source: OU Business School student assignment)

# Extract 2.3

Thrift Bank began as a tiny Belfast banking company called the Thrift Banking Partnership. From the very beginning Thrift catered to the business market and expanded services in line with this need.

Throughout its history, the bank's fortunes have been closely linked with the border counties and Dublin. In 1840, the Bank established its first branch in what is now the Republic of Ireland and significantly expanded the branch network during the 1970s. Following a take-over in the late eighties, these outlets were renamed National Thrift Bank.

Today, Thrift remains the bank of choice for the majority of businesses in Northern Ireland. There are 95 Branches and 11 Business centres. A world-wide network of sister banks provides customers with on-the-spot banking and financial assistance in countries where they wish to conduct business.

Thrift has now been bought out by a Dutch company called 'Utrecht Bank'. The changeover to the new ownership will occur on 18 April 2006.

(Source: OU Business School student assignment)

# Extract 2.4

I work for a charity called Youth Clubs North. The main aim of the charity is to aid young people throughout northern England. This is done primarily through the provision of outdoor education in a residential setting.

The Outdoor Centre, which is called Caxton House Outdoor Centre, is based in Kendal. The Centre has 12 acres of open parkland and lake. This makes it an ideal location to offer young people a taste of the outdoors in a controlled and managed setting.

The residential side of the organisation has developed over the last fourteen years. Throughout that time very little strategic management has taken place. The success of the Centre is mainly through word of mouth and providing an excellent product once the clients have arrived.

In order to improve the ways in which Caxton House operates, it is important that an understanding of how it fits within the wider context of the outdoor education industry be sought. This understanding can then be the basis for producing development plans which can be SMART, Specific, Measurable, Achievable, Realistic, Time related (Drucker, 1999). Through SMART strategic objectives hopefully the organisation can grow and become more efficient and effective at providing an excellent product for its clients.

(Source: OU Business School student assignment)

# Extract 2.5

Liaoning Decoration and Engineering Co. Ltd was founded in 1995. It is a typical SME that employs about 89 staff and with registered capital of about US$3 million. Mr Li, the owner of this company, graduate of Shenyang University, senior construction engineer, is an expert in the construction industry.

This company was set up at the time of reform and open policy in China's economy. At that time, construction in Liaoning province was flourishing, so that with the encouraging policy from the local government, and the limitations of the competitors, this company got the first bucket of gold quickly. Meanwhile Mr Li noticed the lack of excellent import commodities from advanced western countries which attracted the Chinese consumer, and in the construction industry, there were fewer people dealing with high quality and well-designed ceramic products for family use. Mr Li recognised that this is a rather rare chance for himself which would stimulate the development of his business. Therefore, without further inspection of the real market, he decided to invest all his funds in this item. However, as a result of sales problems, there was a big amount of capital restricted by this investment, thus, flow capital and the suitable market has become a pressing issue to solve.

| Text | Notes on how theme links back |
|---|---|
| <u>Liaoning Decoration and Engineering Co. Ltd</u> was founded in 1995. | Theme of the paragraph |
| It is a typical SME that employs about 89 staff and with registered capital of about US$3 million. | Refers to Liaoning Decoration and Engineering Co. Ltd (the first theme) |
| <u>Mr Li, the owner of this company, graduate of Shenyang University, senior construction engineer,</u> is an expert in the construction industry. | New theme but 'this company' refers as above |
| <u>This company</u> was set up at the time of reform and open policy in China's economy. | As above |
| At that time, construction in Liaoning province was flourishing, so that with the encouraging policy from the local government, and the limitations of the competitors, this company got the first bucket of gold quickly. | |
| Meanwhile Mr Li noticed the lack of excellent import commodities from advanced western countries which attracted the Chinese consumer, and in the construction industry, there were fewer people dealing with high quality and well-designed ceramic products for family use. | |
| Mr Li recognised that this is a rather rare chance for himself which would stimulate the development of his business. | |
| Therefore, without further inspection of the real market, he decided to invest all his funds in this item. | |
| However, as a result of sales problems, there was a big amount of capital restricted by this investment, thus, flow capital and the suitable market has become a pressing issue to solve. | |

(Source: student's text)

# Extract 2.6

The Akihabara Electrical Town Association self-describes the Akihabara Electric Town as the World's biggest Electrical Equipment Town, with a collection of about 250 electronics stores (from mega-stores to tiny parts suppliers) concentrated within it, near the Akihabara Station in Central Tokyo. This may be true, since there are no comparable concentrations of electrical shops elsewhere in the world. In its formative years in the 1940s, it was a sort of black market for selling radios and radio parts for the domestic market.

Over the years, as many of the leading Japanese Electronics Companies began using Akihabara as the place to test-launch their latest products, it developed into the place-to-go for electronics enthusiasts and it began to attract enthusiasts from abroad. As the number of overseas visitors increased, many mega stores catering specifically to the needs of tourists have been opened, including duty-free purchase options.

Actually, apart from die-hard enthusiasts, the Electric Town is not well known outside of Japan. With the development of e-commerce, the Electric Town is beginning to lose some of its uniqueness and competitiveness as the place-to-go to find the best electronics products. The Akihabara Electrical Town Association and the Tokyo Metropolitan Government are collaborating to market the Electric Town more aggressively.

| Text | Notes on how theme links back |
|---|---|
| The Akihabara Electrical Town Association self-describes the Akihabara Electric Town as the World's biggest Electrical Equipment Town, with a collection of about 250 electronics stores (from mega-stores to tiny parts suppliers) concentrated within it, near the Akihabara Station in Central Tokyo. | |
| This may be true, since there are no comparable concentrations of electrical shops elsewhere in the world. | |
| In its formative years in the 1940s, it was a sort of black market for selling radios and radio parts for the domestic market. | |
| Over the years, as many of the leading Japanese Electronics Companies began using Akihabara as the place to test-launch their latest products, it developed into the place-to-go for electronics enthusiasts and it began to attract enthusiasts from abroad. | |
| As the number of overseas visitors increased, many mega stores catering specifically to the needs of tourists have been opened, including duty-free purchase options. | |
| Actually, apart from die-hard enthusiasts, the Electric Town is not well known outside of Japan. | |
| With the development of e-commerce, the Electric Town is beginning to lose some of its uniqueness and competitiveness as the place-to-go to find the best electronics products. | |
| The Akihabara Electrical Town Association and the Tokyo Metropolitan Government are collaborating to market the Electric Town more aggressively. | |

(Source: student's text)

# Extract 2.7

## Applying the PESTLE model to my local police force

Political: which party is in power, their views on policing, what is current opinion?

Economic: crime often dependent on money available – shoplifting, theft, burglary – to compensate for low income or wanting what others have (?greed).

Social: background can have impact – poorer neighbourhoods have more low level crime such as vandalism, car theft, broken windows/ fences, etc. Lack of pride in an area can lead to lack of consideration for others and further crimes.

Technological: computer scams/frauds, ways of communicating with others that are harder to trace. Also, positively, databases for recording details – people, vehicles, missing property, DNA, etc., new advanced ways of finding evidence.

Legal: new laws being implemented, old ones adapted.

Environmental: possible changes in government or local authority could lead to new approach. More or different targets to achieve. Terrorist threat, changing priorities.

I considered all three models, STEEP, PEST and PESTLE. All three could be used but I chose PESTLE as it includes Legal. Crime is caused/affected by factors in all areas of the model and the police service is ruled, to varying degrees, by all of them.

(Source: OU Business School student assignment)

# Extract 2.8

## The current situation in the Kazakhstan economy

The current economic growth in Kazakhstan started in mid 1999. As seen from Table 1, GDP at current exchange rates has almost doubled from $16.9 billion in 1999 to $28 billion in 2003. Remarkably the real change in GDP even reached the double digit growth of 12.2% in 2001, which is unprecedented in any other country of the former USSR. The government target for 2002 was the GDP growth of 7.0%. However, it was easily exceeded due to an increase in oil and gas production (17.3%) caused by past investment in the oil extraction sector and improved infrastructure. The decline in population has stopped at a level of 14.8 million people and living standards have significantly improved with GDP per capita raised from £1133 in 1999 to $1820 in 2003. Economic growth and low rate of inflation have significantly reduced the risks of investing in the Kazakhstan economy.

(Source: student's text)

# Extract 2.9

With the development of construction in Beijing and the increase in people's income, many investors are attracted to Beijing, especially to the real estate market because that has become the fastest improving industry. According to the Beijing Statistics Committee, in the first quarter of 2002 there were 1024 new foreign investors approved by government and out of a total investment of 2 billion US dollars, 0.4 billion was invested in the real estate market. As can be seen from the chart, many businesses in Japan and Hong Kong invest in the real estate market in Beijing. This is because of the state of the economies in their countries, and the belief that the price of real estate in Beijing will keep on rising until the 2008 Olympic Games. Nevertheless the chart (Figure 1) shows that by far the largest proportion of investment in the Beijing real estate market comes from North and Latin America, with more than twice the proportion invested by Europe. According to the chart, Chinese investors are only accountable for three-quarters as much as Europeans. These figures suggest a possibly dangerous over-reliance on overseas investment in real estate in Beijing.

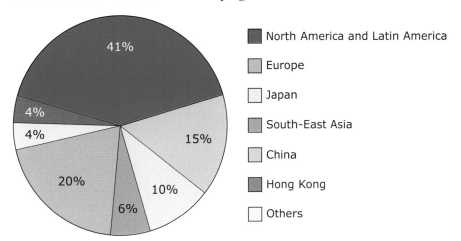

**Figure 1**   Investors in Beijing real estate market by countries and regions

(Source: student's text)

# Text 2.10

In this report I have selected some models and theories to make a description and analysis of my current working environment and the issues confronting it. The usefulness of the models lies in their ability to enable me to articulate that which would otherwise be difficult to express to those without knowledge of the organisation. Theories such as the Systems Map have enabled me to examine issues by providing a frame of reference into which my observations could be placed. Overall, the models and theories have enabled me to understand many of the processes in my organisation together with my roles within it. However it has become clear that no one model perfectly fits a given scenario and that the application of two or more, appropriately modified can achieve a more rounded result overall, and give clear indications for future development and potential.

(Source: Helen Peters)

## Text 2.11

The North Eastern Cooperative (NEC), where I work, is located on the outskirts of Grimsby, offering a cooperative facility for local producers from a wide surrounding radius to exchange and market their products. A number of factors, both local and national, impact on the work of the cooperative. In this report, the aim is to consider the environment in which the NEC seeks to operate, and my role within it. In so doing various business models and theories will be used, to make an analysis of the current situation facing the organisation and its potential for development.

(Source: Helen Peters)

# Session 3 resources

## Text 3.1

### Course learning outcomes for LB160

#### Key communication skills

After completing the course, you will be able to:

- read and summarise written text materials for key points
- communicate effectively in writing in a range of academic and workplace genres, showing recognition of audience and purpose
- select data, information and ideas from different sources and present them in an appropriate fashion to support an argument
- identify some of the strengths and needs of your own communication skills development and identify opportunities to address these
- apply a critical perspective to your own and others' language use.

#### Practical and/or professional skills

After completing the course, you will have developed the skills that you need to:

- analyse business cases and situations to identify problems
- identify and communicate potential solutions based on knowledge of business studies theory, and apply them to your own work situation
- relate the communication skills needed for academic study to those needed in the workplace
- write influential workplace documents.

## Extract 3.2

### The job characteristics model

Hackman and Oldham's (1976, 1980) work on the job characteristics model (JCM) inspired much research into developing a framework for analysing the content of jobs. It looks at the relationship between core job characteristics, employees' psychological states and key outcomes. The model provides a language for talking about the design of jobs within organisations and highlights the complexity of the principles involved.

Hackman and Oldham's model is shown in Figure 3.1.

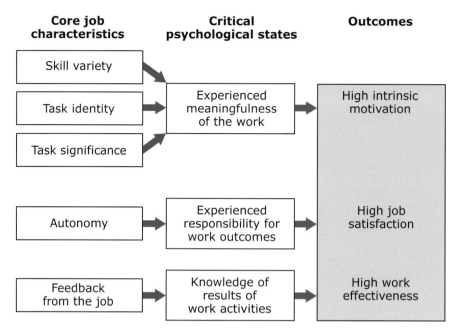

**Figure 3.1** Hackman and Oldham's job characteristics model (Source: Arnold, J., Cooper, C. L. and Robertson, I. T. (1995) *Work Psychology: Understanding Human Behaviour in the Workplace* (2nd edn), London, Pitman. p. 395, Figure 19.1)

## Skill variety

Skill variety is defined as the extent to which a job includes a variety of activities and therefore requires the employee to use a number of different skills and talents. If individuals feel that anyone else could do the work and to as high a standard, they are unlikely to feel any sense of achievement from doing the job. Equally, if doing the job does not utilise their abilities and skills, it is unlikely that they will be learning very much. It may not necessarily be the case that the job offers a lack of skill variety; it may just be that the person is not aware of the skills that are required. On the other hand, jobs that include too much variety are likely to feel fragmented. Employees may find that there are too many different demands on their time and they cannot develop the skills they need to do the job well. It is worth noting that much of the work on job design emerged within an industrial context and, not surprisingly, addressed issues of variety and repetition.

## Task identity

Task identity is about doing a job from beginning to end. It is the extent to which the job requires completion of a whole and identifiable piece of work. It evaluates the degree to which the individual feels involved with the outcomes of their work. In many instances, adding related tasks to a job can increase task identity.

## Task significance

This is defined as the degree to which the job has an impact on the lives or work of other people, whether within the organisation or in the external environment. Some jobs, such as health care and education, have a more obvious impact than others but this is about perception and the extent to which the employee believes his or her job has an impact. In short, if employees can see how their job and contribution fits into the overall picture of achieving the objectives of the business, they are likely to feel more motivated than if they cannot. On this basis, effective communication systems within the business can have a positive effect on task significance.

## Autonomy

This is about the extent to which the job allows the employee to exercise choice in their work. An example of this might be the opportunity to schedule or prioritise work that would give the individual a sense of responsibility for getting the job done.

## Feedback from the job

This is the extent to which the job itself – as opposed to other people – provides information about how the jobholder is performing. This can take the form of, for instance, seeing that an initiative or a change introduced to the job is effective.

In Hackman and Oldham's model, these core job characteristics are said to produce 'critical psychological states'. These are:

- experienced meaningfulness of the work – thought to be influenced by the first three in the list above

- experienced responsibility for outcomes of the work – thought to be influenced by the degree of autonomy and

- knowledge of the actual results of work – affected by feedback from the job.

These in turn are believed to influence motivation, satisfaction and work performance.

Critics of the JCM (for example, Roberts and Glick, 1981) have argued that very few evaluations of the JCM have involved attempts to actually redesign jobs and to see whether the effects of job redesign have been maintained over a long period. However, the JCM has produced a huge amount of research, especially in the USA. It offers a very practical model that suggests that by introducing certain working practices – improving feedback, reviewing responsibilities, combining tasks, forming work groups – the motivating potential of jobs can be increased.

(Source: B120 *An introduction to business studies* (2006) Book 2 *An Introduction to Human Resource Management in Business*, Milton Keynes, The Open University, pp. 21–23)

# Text 3.3

## Anna's self-evaluation

| Text | Stage |
|------|-------|
| Self-evaluation of the following business graduate skill: | |
| Combine information from the Course Reader articles, knowledge and research, and your own experience to illustrate understanding of business concepts. | |
| I was **very pleased** with my efforts at the above skill from the module on Business Processes. While I had found it relatively straightforward to include information from Reader articles and research into my writing, **I had found it much harder to decide** when, where and how much personal experience and knowledge to include. **I had struggled and prevaricated** for quite a while on how to incorporate my own experience into my writing. | Evaluation<br><br>Problem<br><br>Evidence |
| I feel that I was successful in this skill as I found it very easy to relate the module to my own experiences. So, when I was writing Assignment 04, and had an overview of the module, I found it easy to use my own previous work experience in the assignment. At the same time, it was difficult to know how much personal reflection to include, and I was worried that personalising my writing would detract from an attempt at an 'academic' piece of writing. When I am making notes, I try to relate the subject matter to examples from my experience to aid understanding and enable me to remember details, but I was wary of including this in more formal writing. In fact, including my own experience made the essay much easier to write, as I found my writing flowed much better, and by using examples it was easier to explain the points I was trying to make. | |
| Developing my skills in Assignment 04 and the positive feedback received has shown me that personal experience can and should be included in my writing. However, this must also be balanced by the fact that my experience could be limited in certain areas, and it would be easy to make generalisations and assumptions which do not have a wide enough basis. On the other hand, my study has shown me that theories and models can be questioned, and there is no 'right' answer. As I have progressed through the Readers and Study Guide the conflicting views of theorists, combined with my own experience has demonstrated that all viewpoints should be questioned. I feel this is a skill that I need to develop further in my studies, and I need to work on my critical thinking skills. | |
| Even after successfully using this skill for Assignment 04, I am still hesitant to put my own experience into my writing. I found the answer for the self-evaluation in Assignment 06 Part B quite difficult to complete, as I had to put a lot of personal reflection into the self-evaluation. However, it has been a valuable process to reflect on my skills, and the areas of my study that have gone well, and not so well. Time for reflection is not something I normally do (poor time management again!), but the study skills sheets have forced me to think about the skills I have and challenges I face. The fact that I am more aware of my skills and areas that need to be improved will put me in a stronger position in November for my next course. | |

(Source: adapted from OU Business School student assignment)

# Extract 3.4

## Extract from Anna's essay in which she uses personal experience (see particularly the section 'Business Process Re-engineering')

*What are business processes? Critically discuss how they might affect an organisation's ability to compete effectively. (2,500 words)*

## Introduction

Since the 1980s, firms have had to become more focused on their business processes. Business processes are 'transformation processes' that use the resources of people, materials, information, finance and energy for example, as a means of converting inputs into a business into the outputs of goods and services for the consumer. Traditionally, departments and sub-departments within firms were very insular, and performance was measured internally. The business processes approach is a means of transcending the department boundaries so that all function with the customer as the key focus.

[...]

However, the main point to be made about processes is that they vary widely from organisation to organisation, market to market and industry to industry. Competitors in the same market may have very different processes. This is illustrated below when I discuss Porter's value chains. Even though the internal workings of companies vary, they share common processes. The theorists argue that making these processes more streamlined and improving communication between sub-sections of the company will improve efficiency and give firms that follow this approach a competitive advantage in a dynamic market place.

[...]

Business process theory was developed from systems thinking. I will now look at three main theories concerning business processes.

## Stalk

[...]

## Business Process Re-engineering

Hammer and Champy took business processes as being integral to competitive advantage one step further by suggesting that firms should be redesigned around their processes.

Instead of the traditional task approach to business, Hammer and Champy proposed that people were not performing their tasks inefficiently, merely that there was no consideration for the business process. This included, for example, the significance of the task in the business flow and, more importantly, how it impacted on the next task in the business flow. This perspective is in line with the thinking of Stalk and Porter. However, Hammer and Champy took the theory one step further and stated that the logical conclusion was to completely restructure the company so that the flows were followed.

However, the problems associated with this approach immediately struck me as I was reading Hammer, and I identified with Shapiro et al. in their assessment of the difficult practicalities of re-engineering. My last employer installed a new order entry software in the late 1990s that in effect followed a process approach. It was entirely restructuring the tasks that had been performed, creating new job roles and responsibilities. A favourite criticism at the time was of issues 'falling between two chairs', and I recollect the 'charting' exercise that was carried out when the software was being designed. There was considerable tension when implementing the new software, as the consultants were adamant that we had to make as few modifications to the software as possible, and work within its constraints. For the representatives from the sales offices around Europe, the processes that were being imposed bore no relation to actual working practices, and as such were discounted and rejected at every opportunity. It was a common complaint at the time that the only group benefiting from the new software was the consultants, as they earned a small fortune from the company!

After reading the texts by Hammer and Shapiro, the whole process that I had been involved in became very clear, and I understood what the company had been trying to achieve. This reflection then led to the realisation that the process implementation had failed in two major areas. The first was communication, in as much as we did not see the bigger picture. Yes we saw the flow diagrams, but only as far as the problems these would create for our own subsystem flows – not in terms of the overall picture of consumer value added. Secondly, the internal politics in the project hampered the final goal. Regional offices were very protective of their own systems, not wanting to 're-engineer'. With hindsight, I assume that this was due to the lack of communication and an inherent fear that head office would drastically cut jobs in the regional offices.

I agree with Shapiro and his reservations regarding how successful BPR can be. My own experience shows that BPR did not add value within the organisation (however much this buzzword was bandied about), or improve efficiency and effectiveness. The customers certainly did not benefit in the short run. However, in the longer term, the software did have some advantages that allowed us to be more value added in our relationship with the customer, but that was mainly due to the audit trails that the new software provided, making it easier to resolve problems. This is a reactive benefit, in contrast with the proactive benefits of being more process oriented. It did not immediately provide the linkages and smooth flowing processes that would give our firm a competitive advantage. Quite the contrary was true, and many customers were only sympathetic to our inefficiencies as they too were going through a transformation process.

[...]

## Conclusion

[...]

(Source: adapted from OU Business School student assignment)

# Extract 3.5 Models

**Models** – these are *simulations or images* used or constructed by a writer or theorist to provide us with a simplified description of a 'real world' context – such as an economy, a market, a production line or an organisation structure – in which events are occurring which the writer/theorist is trying to explain. They can be presented in the form of a *verbal description*, *a diagram* or sometimes (as in engineering, architecture or design) *a physical construction*. One example you will read about in Section 3 is the 'circular flow of income' model, which is a diagram of an economy (see Reader Chapter 6).

(Source: B200 (2003 *Study Guide 1*, Milton Keynes, The Open University, p. 7)

# Text 3.6

## Sandy's reflection on using models and diagrams in business studies

I have particularly focused on the skill of using models to describe business environments. This is because my skill level was initially low as I had little experience of using models. Use of models in previous study had only been to describe situations, rather than analyse or synthesise.

This skill was developed early through application of models in Assignment 02. However, it became clear that the use of models was imperative throughout all four modules and so I sought to develop this beyond the skills audit undertaken after the environments module. I have developed the use of information technology to support this skill as it enabled me to demonstrate my understanding of models.

In Assignment 01, I used Ansoff's product/market grid (Figure 1) to describe Nike's growth strategy:

|  | Current products | New products |
|---|---|---|
| Current markets | Market penetration | Product development |
| New markets | Market development | Diversification |

**Figure 1** Ansoff's product/market grid

In Assignment 02, this was developed by using a more complex model, that of Mintzberg's cast of players (Figure 2). This described and supported analysis of Nike's stakeholders.

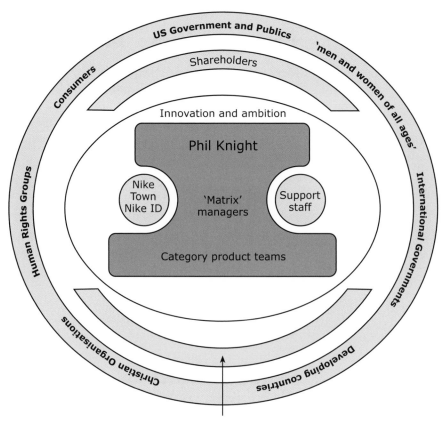

**Figure 2** Mintzberg's cast of players

I then took Coates' economy model (Figure 3) and developed this to present and simulate part of the economy of a developing country, again stretching my understanding of IT to present a concept clearly.

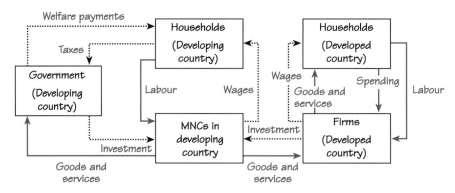

**Figure 3** Coates' economy model

Further examples of using models are at pages 39 and 41. Non-pictorial presentation of models was also developed in Assignment 03. My preparation for this is at pages 17–21.

By practising using models and stretching my intellectual understanding and application of them, I have developed a high level of skill in this area, which I believe to be a fundamental aspect of business studies because models make complex ideas fathomable and theories applicable.

This culminated in Assignment 05 when I had the confidence to attempt my own model to show a relationship between levels of control in bureaucratic organisations and the level of creativity and innovation (see Figure 4). Although my tutor refined the model slightly, it received 'excellent' feedback:

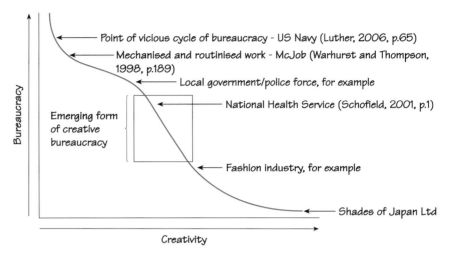

**Figure 4** My own model

Although I was able to effectively develop this skill, it was not always done with a structured plan and I think this would have focused my attention on improving even more this aspect of my work and may have resulted in a better mark for the later assignment.

The development of my skill with models has complemented the development of a wide range of other skills such as using different methods of communication and using diagrammatic representation.

To further improve my use of models, I need to develop a more accurate method of creating models so that their application can be reliable. In some of the business journal articles that I am now reading (p. 52), I have found that much empirical and statistical research is undertaken during the development of models. Over the next two to three years, I will research how to undertake sound academic research to support the development of original theories and hypotheses. My tutor has suggested that I use spreadsheet software for business data analysis (p. 32). At my next personal development review in my workplace, I intend to discuss with my manager in-house training options for this.

# Text 3.7

## Sandy's skills portfolio front page and contents page

CONTENTS

SANDY CHANG

UNDERSTANDING BUSINESS
BEHAVIOUR

SKILLS PORTFOLIO

Sandy's front page and contents page

# Extract 3.8

## Opening sentences

(a)  The skills area that I have chosen to concentrate on is 'recognise and use different strategies for achieving targets'.

(b)  The business graduate skill I want to discuss is, using models to describe and explain the business environment.

(c)  The skill I have decided to look at is 'Take notes to summarise information for tutor marked assignments and examination preparation' from the Environments module.

(d)  Being fairly new to academic study, there were many areas where improvement was required to become a successful learner. I decided to focus on 'Taking notes and summarising information in preparation for Assignments and later examination'.

(e)  My greatest weakness is in using models and diagrams and this was the skill with which I chose to work.

(f)  One area that I considered to be weak with my study was the ability to organise my note taking in such a way that I could then use the notes effectively to structure and complete an assignment of recognisable quality.

# Extract 3.9

## Nouns or noun groups to refer to skills

(a)  Being able to simplify descriptions of models enabled me to progress on to understanding theories.

(b)  I found using mind maps very useful when planning essays.

(c)  Studying the diagrams presented in the Readers has assisted me in understanding the material presented.

(d)  Making more use of flow charts to show processes should make studying easier and assist in note taking.

(e)  The three stages of extracting key points, sorting them into logical groups and developing sentences from the key points enabled me to plan and organise the points extracted from the chapters.

(f)  At this stage of my study I am not aware of any other methods for planning and organising written work so I cannot assess if a different method suits my study work.

(g)  However, ensuring that sufficient referencing details were logged with the notes would have further improved the strategy by preventing the frustration of searching back through Readers and previous notes to find the correct page details.

(h)  I identified planning and organising at Skills Audit 2 as an important set of skills for me to work on in the context of Business Studies, and tried to work on it from several angles at every opportunity. Lack of discipline was the learning skills weakness I chose to focus on.

(i)  Assignment 05 was my first attempt at organising the material into sections marked by headings and subheadings.

# Texts 3.10–3.14

## Self-evaluations of skills with using models and diagrams

The sample student reports presented here should not be seen as ideal examples of self-evaluation reports. They did achieve reasonably high grades in their courses, but they are not necessarily perfect. A self-evaluation report is personal to the writer and these samples are presented here to stimulate **your** thinking about **your** self-evaluation report.

You should also note that these reports deal with using business models and diagrams in business writing. The first three focus on using models. The next two deal with using diagrams.

# Text 3.10

*Choose one of these skills and in a statement of not more than 500 words:*

1  *Explain what you did to improve in your chosen skill area.*
2  *Analyse the effectiveness of your approach. (Could a different strategy have resulted in further improvements?)*
3  *Identify any further work you could undertake to improve in this area (you should mention sources of support which you might use, for example study skills books) and explain how this could make up part of your strategy for future study.*

## Using models to describe the business environment

My greatest weakness is in using models and diagrams and this was the skill with which I chose to work. Unfortunately, due to unforeseen time pressure, I was not able to work with this skill area as much as I had intended, but I have started to try to work with it more and intend to continue to do so.

In order to improve with this skill, I first had to force myself to actually look at the models used in the course material instead of just skimming over them as I normally do. I found that I had to slow down and try to understand the models to see what they represented and then consider how this might have been represented simply in words. I began to realise that models are useful and can actually simplify ideas and relationships.

Although this strategy was a good beginning, I could have devoted more time to doing this. I could also have compared the model with a text I actually wrote instead of merely thinking about it. This would have made me even more aware of the advantages of modelling. Additionally, I could also have tried to make more models and visual representations of my own. Further, I misunderstood that in the field of business studies it is perfectly legitimate, and even recommended, to use models and diagrams in an essay so I could have used models more in my assignments, especially in the assignment on processes, which would have given me more practice and anchored the concept more firmly in my mind.

In order to improve in this area, I need to stop and study the models and visual representations in the articles I read. For example, when I proof-read the work of colleagues, I should actually look at their diagrams instead of merely reading their words. I could also start to use models in my teaching. Not only could students describe the models in their own words, but it should even be possible to find texts which they can answer in the form of models and flow charts instead of as summaries or as reading comprehensions. This would be a very useful way for me to work with my visualising skills, giving me ideas and input from many sources and it would also generate good discussion in class. Moreover, I also believe that many of my students would find it an interesting and rewarding way to study language and, in many cases, I think that they would better understand and retain not only the content but also the language of the article, if we were to sometimes vary our approach and work in this way.

Before I begin to do this, however, I need to study models more thoroughly. I need to work more actively with the models provided in the course material and begin to use the large selection of books on business and economics to which I have access and which I can use for this purpose.

(Source: OU Business School student assignment)

# Text 3.11

*Choose one of these skills and in a statement of not more than 500 words:*

1  *Explain what you did to improve in your chosen skill area.*

2  *Analyse the effectiveness of your approach. (Could a different strategy have resulted in further improvements?)*

3  *Identify any further work you could undertake to improve in this area (you should mention sources of support which you might use, for example study skills books) and explain how this could make up part of your strategy for future study.*

## Using models to describe the business environment

1  In the Environment module, I focused on the skill of 'using models to describe business environments' as noted on skills audit 1 review form on page A-10 to A-11. In this module we were introduced to new methods for identifying key factors and analysing these in depth. The tools were models, concepts and theories. This module was mainly concerned with using models to examine the business environment. It provided a good basis for the comparison of models which we were expected to do in later modules.

2      The Study Guide summarised the meanings of the terms *concepts*, *models* and *theories* (pg. A-30). This gave me a clear understanding and definition for each term. At tutorials, the models were discussed in small groups, broken down into more manageable explanations in our own words, and presented back to the whole tutorial group for review and discussion. I used mind maps (referring to the book, *How to Mind Map*, by Tony Buzan) to capture the main elements and provide a clear picture of the model.

I found that attending tutorials along with working through examples enabled me to understand how to interpret models and to apply the models in my own words in Assignment 02. My tutor noted on skills audit 1 review form that there was 'excellent learning displayed in this area, good use of models' (pg. A-11) and on Assignment 02 that I had a 'very good understanding of the model' (pg. A-14).

As I progressed through the next module, I used the same method of learning and found that this was very successful and allowed me to analyse differences between models. My tutor noted on Assignment 03 that I 'demonstrated a sound understanding of the four models, their similarities and differences' and also 'explored how the models offer both competing and complementary perspectives on how markets function' (pg. A-52). I believe I was competent in explaining the main elements of the four models and, as noted by my tutor on Assignment 03, I presented a 'good page which gives the key fruits of the four models' (pg. A-55). I believe that my approach to understanding models was successful and delivered the results in my Assignments (pg. A-14 and A-52).

I also found that my work on models enabled me to understand theories and use them in Assignment 04 (pg. A-71 to A-79). My tutor noted that my Assignment 'was a thorough appreciation of the theory and related issues' (pg. A-71) and my arguments were 'cogent and well structured and discussed the range of material offered on the course'.

3      I plan on using a similar strategy for future study to ensure I continue to develop my understanding. I aim to improve in this area by referring to *The Good Study Guide* (Northedge) and *Good Essay Writing* (Redman). Both books provide useful information about using models and theories for completing assignments. This course has provided me with a clearer understanding of working with concepts, models and theories and this will be a useful skill for my future courses.

(Source: OU Business School student assignment)

# Text 3.12

*Choose one of these skills and in a statement of not more than 500 words:*

1   *Explain what you did to improve in your chosen skill area.*

2   *Analyse the effectiveness of your approach. (Could a different strategy have resulted in further improvements?)*

3   *Identify any further work you could undertake to improve in this area (you should mention sources of support which you might use, for example study skills books) and explain how this could make up part of your strategy for future study.*

## Using models to describe the business environment

The business graduate skill I want to discuss is using models to describe and explain the business environment. This concept was studied mainly in module one of the course, using Mintzberg's stakeholder model and the STEP model, both of which cover key areas in the business world. (See Assignment 02 Q1 for examples on the Nike case.)

Studying these two models early in the course helped me to understand the various factors that businesses have to deal with in both the near and far environments, i.e. at home in the UK and globally. The Nike case showed how social, technological, economic and political issues have to be adhered to and how important these factors are in the business environment.

But my essays seemed to lack good arguments, structure and flow when trying to describe these models, according to comments from my tutor. In feedback from Skills Audit 1, my tutor suggested I should include diagrams to assist explanations in my essays. This made sense to me as I realised I could have used the Mintzberg face model in Assignment 02 to help show the various stakeholders at play in a business environment. So to improve in this skill area I included the 'circular flow model' in Assignment 03, Markets, and the 'value chain' model in Assignment 04, Processes. (See examples in Evidence section.) So, by adopting this different learning and writing strategy, I have learned that using diagrams in an essay can help the reader understand certain points of the argument.

But to improve further in this area I need to do more essays! In studying my next course, *Managing in the workplace*, I hope to gain more experience in this area. As part of my ongoing attempts to improve my study skills, I purchased and started to use mind map software to help me organise the way I work. I have also purchased *The Good Study Guide* which I intend to use as a support source for future study. But I realise these skills will only improve with practice, by understanding what the course is trying to present, and by thinking about the feedback given by the tutors on my assignments.

(Source: OU Business School student assignment)

# Text 3.13

*Choose one of these skills and in a statement of not more than 500 words:*

1    *Explain what you did to improve in your chosen skill area.*

2    *Analyse the effectiveness of your approach. (Could a different strategy have resulted in further improvements?)*

3    *Identify any further work you could undertake to improve in this area (you should mention sources of support which you might use, for example study skills books) and explain how this could make up part of your strategy for future study.*

## Prepare material which represents information diagrammatically

### 1  Explain what you did to improve in your chosen skill area

For Assignment 04 (Skills Audit Review 3) I researched Nike and my employer (ALCO), obtaining information relating to their structure, business processes and value chain, to enable me to illustrate the similarities and differences between them and their sub-units/ departments. Not being very confident with Excel, I input the information in such a way that it would clearly illustrate Nike's and ALCO's sub-units, and did this in the form of graphs, deciding on the best graph to use. I played about with the graph display and settled for the pie-chart, each colour indicating a different department/sub-unit. I was happy with the outcome.

I then produced Transformation Models illustrating Nike's and ALCO's inputs and outputs, by way of a table (which I note from my tutor's comments could have been better illustrated as a diagram with arrows, which I agree with).

I wanted to provide a lot of information about Nike's value chain and felt the best way to provide this would be to illustrate it using Porter's model of the value chain from p. 56 of the Reader. I used Porter's diagram as a template onto which I input my interpretation of Nike's processes, various direct and indirect support and primary activities, infrastructure, and quality assurance activities. As the information was complex, I felt presenting it in diagrammatic form would help me (and my tutor) clearly see the vast amount of information I had obtained at a glance, making it easier to understand.

1.1 Evidence: Appendix 4 (Nike's value chain and graphs in Assignment 04).

### 2  Analyse the effectiveness of your approach. (Could a different strategy have resulted in further improvements?)

I believe the diagram I produced showing Nike's value chain (see Appendix 4) was appropriate due to the complex nature of the information I was illustrating. I believe my approach, converting Porter's diagram, creating a template, transferring Nike's information onto it worked well and was clearly referenced.

I believe my approach to the Transformation Model (see Appendix 4) could have been better, as suggested by my tutor. In retrospect, I see it was inappropriate as it didn't 'read' well, could have been clearer and the list of inputs/outputs would have been shorter.

I believe the graphs I produced (see Appendix 4) illustrating Nike's and my employer's sub-units/departments were clear and easy to understand and, therefore, I feel it was appropriate.

**3 *Identify any further work you could undertake to improve in this area (mention sources of support you might use, for example study skill books) and explain how this could make up part of your strategy for future study.***

I obtained Toolkit 3 'Working with charts, graphs and tables' (K. Gilmartin and K. Rex) which I am finding helpful. I have also been looking back through the diagrams provided in the Course Readers and modules, to obtain ideas, improve my technique and aid my understanding.

Prior to starting the course, *Managing in the workplace*, I intend to access e-resources via the OU website/homepage to read up on the course content, setting myself some exercises based on the course concepts. I am also using Excel at work to provide monthly figures for my manager, which is boosting my confidence. I intend to continue using spider (and any other) diagrams while note-taking, which should further improve my confidence. I expect the course website to provide advice and links regarding diagramming also.

(Source: OU Business School student assignment)

# Text 3.14

*Choose one of these skills and in a statement of not more than 500 words:*

1   *Explain what you did to improve in your chosen skill area.*
2   *Analyse the effectiveness of your approach. (Could a different strategy have resulted in further improvements?)*
3   *Identify any further work you could undertake to improve in this area (you should mention sources of support which you might use, for example study skills books) and explain how this could make up part of your strategy for future study.*

## Prepare material which represents information diagrammatically

In the processes module I focused on the skill 'Using diagrammatic representation to organise large amounts of information and aid understanding'. In the past I have used straightforward note taking and highlighting of areas to record relevant information, however I often find these hard to trace back to in a hurry and they do not always fully clarify a point. I have found that by using diagrams and tables as part of my note taking I am able to understand large quantities of information. In using diagrams I can cross-reference the information given in the course material to the diagram itself and better see how it relates to other aspects of a model or theory. I now take more time studying diagrams as I realise they often show a lot of information and I re-create them for my note taking or for use in essays.

I think this has been one of the most effective areas I could have focused on, as it has helped not only in my note taking but also my understanding of certain subjects and the writing of the assignments. I also expect it to help me in my exam revision. I had used some diagrams in essays before, to support an argument but it is only recently that I have realised their effectiveness as a study tool. I think this was a good area to focus on and I don't know that there was another area which I would have got so much from; I think this has been supported by the good grades I have continued to achieve. As an example, I found the Value Chain initially quite hard to understand, but I found through following the course material and creating one myself that I understood it better.

Another form of diagrammatic note taking that I could improve in would be the use of mind maps. This is something that has been promoted throughout my studies with The Open University, however it is something that I have yet to use effectively. The Open University does have some good support material and related books on using these kinds of skills and this is something I shall be looking into before the start of my next course, I think that seeing how effective the diagrams and tables have been to my study that I will make more of an effort to use visual aids to study and revise with. It would also help to have a better computer package that would enable me to draw diagrams on my computer.

I will endeavour in my future courses to use more diagrams, tables and mind maps to not only help me with understanding the course work but also to help with writing of essays, finding relevant notes easier and with the subsequent exam. I will also endeavour to keep using the diagrams in my assignments as I did for Assignment 02 in which we were asked to analyse the Stakeholder Model for Nike. I found by re-creating the model, it helped me support my analysis of the company and would help anyone reading it also understand my analysis. This has been submitted as part of my evidence in my portfolio.

Reference: Mayle, D. and Barnes, D. (2003) 'Business processes and organisational success', *Understanding Business Behaviour: Processes*, The Open University, Milton Keynes.

(Source: OU Business School student assignment)

# Text 3.15

## Student A

### Graduate skill development

*Plan and organise written work in the context of business studies*

One area that I considered to be weak with my study was the ability to organise my note taking in such a way that I could then use the notes effectively to structure and complete an Assignment of recognisable quality. My standard method was to extract notes from the text and then go back over the notes when writing an Assignment. The problem with this was that throughout the chapters of the Reader there would be key points in one chapter that could be linked to points raised in another. Although my standard method would identify and extract key points it had no process within in it to group key points together. Therefore, I would either miss points that were related when writing an Assignment or not identify a relationship between points raised in different chapters or paragraphs.

A skill that I found particularly useful to correct this problem was addressed in the 'Markets' module. By completing Activity 3.3 (as shown on page 15) in this module I was able to improve the skill to plan and organise written work. This activity puts into practice the three stage approach outlined in activity 3.1 and applying the method to Assignment 03 really showed me how useful and valuable it is. The three stages of extracting key points, sorting them in to logical groups and developing sentences from the key points enable planning and organisation of the points extracted from the chapters covered throughout the module.

I applied this method when writing Assignment 03 (as shown on pages 16–20) and I found that it helped greatly with ensuring that relevant points were included in the Assignment and, importantly, that they were included in a logical manner so that the Assignment was reasonably structured. Taking time to apply the first two stages of this method has really benefited my study and allowed me to produce pieces of work which have structure and flow from one chapter to another, something that I feel was missing from previous work. Having realised the value of this approach (my Assignment score significantly improved) and the improvement it brought to my written work I applied it when creating plans and writing both Assignment 04 and Assignment 05.

At this stage of my study I am not aware of any other methods for planning and organising written work so I cannot assess if a different method suits my study work. However, I am happy that this three stage method provides me with a skill that improves the quality of work that I produce so I will use it during future study and during my working day.

I do not profess to be an expert at extracting points from text and organising them into a logical form to help plan an Assignment but I feel that the more I practise this skill the easier it will be for me to produce work of an improved quality. Being able to plan and organise written work is something that has developed as this course has progressed and I am confident that it is a skill which I will rely upon.

(Source: OU Business School student assignment)

# Text 3.16

## Student B

### Graduate skill development

*Taking notes and summarising information in preparation for assignments and examination*

The skill I have decided to look at is 'Take notes to summarise information for tutor marked assignments and examination preparation' from the Environments module. At the beginning of the course after I had watched the video on Nike I made rough notes which I tried to follow later. When I looked at the notes they did not really make a lot of sense. I watched the video again and made more structured notes, taking my time and stopping the video at certain points to carry on with the notes. I watched the video three times to make sure I had understood the main points.

To improve in this skill area I have changed my approach to note taking and to summarise information for the assignments. I now compile rough notes at the beginning of a module and skim-read the module. I then read through the module and the Study Guide, completing the activities and making notes of what I believe to be the most important concepts. I use a combination of the Readers, the Study Guide, *The Good Study Guide* and the World Wide Web to help with my note making. For examination preparation I read through the specimen examination paper at the beginning of the course. I also take at least two weeks off work in October and go back to the beginning of the course, rereading the Study Guide and the Readers and taking notes on anything I may have missed previously which I feel is important. During the last month of the course, I read questions from the specimen exam paper, put all my references away, time myself for forty minutes and try to answer the questions. This approach worked very well on my previous course.

One of the most useful activities I have found in this course was Activity 3.1 from the Markets module which showed how to extract the key points from an article when trying to answer questions. I now try to use this strategy all the time for answering tutor-marked assignments and organising notes as I read through the Study Guide and Readers.

I have found the key points approach really effective.

To improve in this area I intend to follow this approach in conjunction with my own index of the chapters and the calendars I have used. For future study when I am note taking for an examination I will condense my notes. Rather than copying vast amounts of text, I will use bullet points, single words or phrases or a diagram to recall a course concept or idea.

I have found some of the text in the Readers quite difficult to follow but I have managed to pick out some relevant points and bullet them to jog my memory.

For future study I will use a combination of all the different note-making techniques I have learned on this course.

(Source: OU Business School student assignment)

# Text 3.17

## Critically examine Wal-Mart's attempts at managing its culture in international contexts.

One way of thinking about the culture of an organisation is as its personality or identity. Culture is inherently intangible. Culture is recognised as a significant factor in the way organisations and the people who work within them behave. It is increasingly claimed to be one of the most important influences on organisational success and failure. A simplistic view of culture is 'the way we do things around here'.

A clearer definition of culture is 'the collection of traditions, values, policies, beliefs, and attitudes that constitute a pervasive context for everything we do and think in an organisation' (McLean and Marshall, 1993) or 'A pattern of shared and stable beliefs and values that are developed within a company across time' (Needle, 1989).

Wilson and Rosenfeld suggest that culture manifests itself as 'the basic values, ideologies and assumptions which guide and fashion individual and business behaviour. These values are evident in more tangible factors such as stories, rituals, language and jargon, office decoration and layout and prevailing modes of dress among the staff" (Wilson and Rosenfeld, 1990).

There is little doubt that Wal-Mart has a power culture. The organisation is very much like a club; it exists to enable the decisions of those at the centre to be carried out. The culture is dominated by a charismatic founder, Sam Walton. Here personality is more important than formal structures, roles or procedures in sustaining and advancing the organisation.

Admittedly Wal-Mart has made mistakes with its lack of cultural sensitivity in the UK, Germany, Argentina and Japan but they are after all the largest retail chain, the largest company and the biggest employer in the world. It is perhaps expecting a bit too much for a company to be one hundred per cent perfect in all of its operations.

Many of the cultural problems associated with Wal-Mart appear to stem from their anti-union stance. This has created problems in the UK where a strike was recently called off at the last minute and in Germany there have been problems with German labour laws and other aspects of government legislation. When Wal-Mart moved into Germany, the official company remained English. American managers made no attempt to learn German and this created serious communication problems with German-speaking staff.

This was bound to cause cultural conflict and appears to be an own goal by Wal-Mart. Perhaps this culture clash and inability to negotiate with the German trade unions contributed to Wal-Mart's decision to abandon its operation in Germany.

Wal-Mart admits to having an aggressive vision and commitment to change. A commitment to change would infer a change in culture. With Wal-Mart operating a global company, they encounter a range of cultural problems. There is a language barrier; this has been seen with the problems in Germany. Other problems they may encounter are possible religious barriers, however the company have been aware of this and showed their cultural awareness by selling Ramadan calendars with chocolate treats for children in areas with significant Muslim populations.

It must be extremely difficult for Wal-Mart to manage its organisational culture because of the huge scale of its international operations. Different countries' employees will have different values, languages and perceptions that they bring to their workplace and to their commitment to the Wal-Mart organisation. There will always be a variety of cultures and subcultures in any organisation. Wal-Mart need to realise that different countries have different cultural values. It appears that Wal-Mart try to instil the American culture in their international operations. It is highly unlikely that the American way is going to be a success in countries such as Germany, Argentina or even the UK.

There are instances of Wal-Mart not being culturally sensitive in other countries but they appear to learn quickly from their mistakes. Wal-Mart has many critics and there are dedicated anti-Wal-Mart websites who protest about low wages, cheap foreign labour, environmental issues and that fact that Wal-Mart seem to steamroller into a country and drive out local traders. Wal-Mart, because of its size, is really there to be shot at.

Culture may not be at the top of Wal-Mart's priority list: they may well be more interested in technology, the product market or, more importantly, making a profit.

(Source: OU Business School student assignment)

# Text 3.18

## Critically examine Wal-Mart's attempts at managing its culture in international contexts.

The effect of corporate culture on a business is one thing that is not easily measured because, unlike size or financial figures, it is not tangible. Like most large organisations, Wal-Mart has obtained and moulded its own corporate culture. In the following paragraphs I will examine what this culture is and how it has affected the multinational nature of the organisation.

Corporate culture is all about establishing values that are applied to the running of an organisation with the aim of creating a cohesive unit and is the product of multiple factors such as company goals, structure, size and ownership. The culture of an organisation sets the basis from which strategy is determined and culture change can be used by management of a company to achieve improved performance.

Because culture, through the adoption of values, provides emotional engagement and a method for organisational members to identify with the organisation, it is a powerful tool used by companies to encourage commitment and promote enthusiasm in its employees.

The culture adopted by any organisation is dynamic; it is something that develops over time and generally changes as the business itself alters. Culture is not uniform, different organisations have different cultures and these differences are considered when explaining performance differences between organisations, particularly those that operate within the same market sector. Wal-Mart has a distinctive corporate culture based upon the principles applied by Sam Walton, the company founder. The Wal-Mart culture is based upon strong values which are endorsed and passed down from senior management.

A main factor in the Wal-Mart culture is the goal of keeping operating costs to a minimum so that savings can be passed on to the customer in the form of lower prices. Examples of the company frugality (i.e. sharing of hotel rooms) and drive for efficiency (i.e. supply chain logistics performance) are provided in the case study and show how the culture is in existence to maintain customer satisfaction.

Wal-Mart managers were expected to be highly visible and operate an 'open door' policy which encouraged managers to spend time in the stores and improve the flow of communication by sharing information. This allows staff to provide initiatives for improving sales which may include opportunities to explore local ethnic diversity.

The Wal-Mart culture has been instrumental in its expansion into countries outside of the USA. The values that Wal-Mart adopted to make it the largest retailer in the USA were applied when it expanded into Mexico, Germany, etc. However, not all of the cultural concepts which it introduced in its foreign stores were readily accepted by the employees, the customer or the local authorities. For example, Wal-Mart had developed a slogan which its employees chant each morning known as the 'Wal-Mart Cheer'; this was met with opposition in Germany with staff who were uncomfortable with its existence.

There were other failures experienced by Wal-Mart in Germany which highlighted how corporate culture needs to be sensitive towards national diversity. Wal-Mart managers failed to realise that, by continuing to use English as the primary language in company communications and not attempting to converse in German, they were excluding German-speaking staff.

Having learned from its experiences in Germany, Wal-Mart adopted a different approach with its takeover of Asda in the UK. Wal-Mart had realised that to apply its culture there would be change to an already established business. To ease the process, Wal-Mart used a consulting firm to communicate the changes and introduce the culture to senior Asda staff, who then promoted it throughout the business.

As mentioned previously, a function of the Wal-Mart corporate culture is to keep costs low and maintain customer satisfaction. The culture also exists to preserve staff loyalty and commitment. In 2002, with 1.6 million staff, Wal-Mart was the world's biggest employer. However, employees were not referred to as staff but as 'associates', signifying that they all had an equal part to play in the success of the Wal-Mart 'family', another term used to illustrate the culture of belonging and involvement. Part of the 'Wal-Mart Cheer' performed by staff each day asks the question 'Whose Wal-Mart is it?' with the answer 'My Wal-Mart'. Despite the benefits of the terminology to create a sense of emotional engagement, there have been criticisms of how Wal-Mart has created a cult-like culture with staff being referred to as 'Wal-Martians'.

Despite the problems of transferring the corporate culture outside the USA, Wal-Mart has learned from its mistakes and has taken a fresh approach to culture development in other countries. There are many benefits to the company and its employees by having a distinct culture and the management of this will ensure that the values, instilled by Sam Walton at the beginning, will continue for many years.

(Source: student assignment, OU Business School)

# Session 4 resources

## Text 4.1

Hi Pete

Just heard about your promotion. Congratulations! I expect we'll see you in a fancy car soon. Make sure you don't get too big for your boots and park it in the boss's space!

I'm busy working on the revision of the document you sent. Hope to have it ready soon. Any urgency?

See you later.

Adam

## Text 4.2

Dear Peter

Thank you for sending me the report on the Telecoms document for revision.

I am pleased to inform you that we have started work on the revision and that we fully expect to be able to send it to you by the end of the week.

In our earlier discussions, you mentioned that you were facing some tight deadlines. In view of this, it may be possible for us to send the revised version to you before the agreed deadline of Friday. If you would like us to do this, please let me know as soon as possible and I will take the necessary steps to make sure that it is completed and returned to you on Thursday. Should this not be necessary, we will make sure that you receive the document on Friday.

Finally, I understand from the newsletter that you have received a promotion. I would like to take this opportunity to offer you my congratulations. I wish you every success in your new position.

I look forward to hearing from you if you decide the report is needed on Thursday.

Best wishes

Adam Owen-Smith

# Session 5 resources

(Source: NatWest Travel Service, 2007)

## Text 5.1

# Tantalising Offers to Whet Your Appetite

From family fun in the UK, sunny holidays in the Med and great fun afloat to the glitz of the USA

### Holiday Savings, All Year Round!

With the NatWest Travel Service, you can take advantage of savings on holidays taken any time of the year, to destinations all around the world. And as the club is operated by Thomas Cook – the original travel experts – you are guaranteed expert travel advice and an efficient, friendly service.

- 10% discount on any Thomas Cook, jmc and Sunset holidays until 31st October 2007
- 6% discount on holidays with more than 150 tour operators. Please refer to terms and conditions overleaf for exceptions
- Specially negotiated fares with more than 50 top airlines
- Discounted hotel rates
- No credit card fee when you pay with your NatWest Credit Card (usually 2.25% charge, up to a maximum of £50)

### Save 10% on Thomas Cook, jmc and Sunset holidays!

Book a Thomas Cook, jmc or Sunset holiday with us now and you'll save 10% off the latest cost of your holiday - that's in addition to any tour operator funded savings and even applies to late deal prices!

So whether you're looking for a last-minute bargain, planning your winter getaway or getting prepared for summer 2008, get booking now and save yourself even more with the NatWest Travel Service.

*Thomas Cook  jmc  Sunset*

For a holiday quote or to find out more, call the NatWest Travel Service on

## 0870 752 0927

Open 8am to 10pm, 7 days a week. Please quote ref. NW3

### ✓ Save £50 PLUS 10% off Cyprus holidays

Plan your summer 2008 holiday now for the best availability and early booking deals around.

Choose a Thomas Cook, jmc or Sunset holiday to Cyprus travelling on selected dates next summer and receive a £50 bonus discount per booking, in addition to your 10% travel service discount and any tour operator funded early booking offers available when you book.

Offer ends 31st October 2007.

*Thomas Cook  jmc  Sunset*

### ✓ Save up to £100 on Hoseasons holidays

With over 12,000 places to stay in Britain, Ireland and Europe, Hoseasons is the UK's leading self-catering specialist. Book ANY Hoseasons holiday this month and make fantastic savings!

| Holiday Cost | Discount |
|---|---|
| Spend up to £199 | 6% |
| Spend £200 – £349 | £25 |
| Spend £350 – £699 | £50 |
| Spend £700 – £999 | £75 |
| Spend £1,000+ | £100 |

Offer ends 31st October 2007.

*Hoseasons*

### ✓ Cruise the Caribbean from only £1035

Island hop around the Caribbean this winter onboard Ocean Village Two and you can forget the timetables of conventional cruises as you experience a different way to holiday.

Plus, our exclusive offer gives you up to 50% off the brochure price!

**Coral & Calypso / Sugar & Spice**
Departing UK: 16 January 2008
Fly to Barbados, sail to Tortola,
St Maarten, St Kitts, Antigua, Dominica,
Barbados, Isla Margarita, Grenada,
St Lucia, Martinique, St Vincent,
Barbados. Fly to UK.

Exclusive price starts from just £1,035 per person

Offer ends 31st October 2007.

*ocean VILLAGE*  the cruise for people who don't do cruises

### ✓ £100 off USA breaks with Virgin Holidays

Jet off to the states with Virgin Holidays for up to 5 nights on a city break (including a Saturday night stay) and receive £100 per couple bonus discount, in addition to your 6% travel service discount.

Choose from New York, Boston, Washington DC, Chicago, Las Vegas, Los Angeles and San Francisco, departing 01 January – 20 March or 28 March – 30 November 2008.

Prices start from just £457 per person based on a 3-night stay at the Comfort Inn Revere in Boston.

Offer ends 24th October 2007.

*Virgin HOLIDAYS*

Please see reverse for terms and conditions that apply to these offers.

# Text 5.2

Current Accounts

# Telephone Banking

## Using a telephone
## 'I do everything else by phone, why not my banking too?'

No access to the internet, or no time to visit a branch? And maybe picking up the phone comes more naturally when you're trying to get things done. Then you need to know about Barclays Telephone Banking. It's quick, it's easy and it's available 24 hours a day, 365 days a year.[††]

Off shopping? Why not call and find out your balance so you know what you can afford to spend. Just remembered you haven't paid your credit card? Do it now while it's still fresh in your mind. It really is that simple with Barclays Telephone Banking. With a push-button phone your accounts and all of our other services are literally at your fingertips, any time of day. And if you need more than a fast automated service, that's OK too – because our advisers are available from 7am to 11 pm, seven days a week.

[††] Telephone banking availability excludes scheduled maintenance or inaccessibility due to factors/events outside our control.

With Telephone Banking you can:
- Access statement info
- Make Barclaycard bill payments
- Transfer money between your Barclays accounts
- Change your passcode to a memorable number
- Hear your balance
- Enquire about your other Barclays accounts
- Apply for other Barclays products such as a savings account or a loan

You can take advantage of Telephone Banking by calling 0845 7 555 555,[**] by speaking to a Personal Banker or visiting our website www.barclays.com

[**]Calls to 0845 numbers will costs no more than 4p per minute, minimum call charge 5.5p (current at September 2006) for BT customers. The price on non-BT phone lines may be different. Calls may be monitored for training and security purposes.

(Source: Barclays Bank, 2006)

# Text 5.3

# Online Banking

## Using the internet
## 'My life's so busy I really need a bank that's always open

Stuck at your office desk, but need to pay some bills? No problem. Want to arrange an overdraft on a bank holiday? That's easy too. With Barclays Online Banking, banking hours are a thing of the past. You'll still keep bang up to date with your account because all online transactions will be shown on your statement as usual.

Of course, if you do have time to visit your branch or give us a call, we'll be pleased to speak to you.

### The nuts and bolts of net banking
If you have a Current Account and Connect Card you can do the following online:

- Access your statement instantly – you can even choose a range of dates
- Sort out bills as soon as they arrive. You tell us the company's name and your reference number and we make the payment whenever you want
- Transfer money to any UK bank account
- Set up, amend or cancel regular payments
- Set up or apply to increase an overdraft
- Apply for a loan. If your application is approved the money can be in your account in three hours
- Open an e-Savings Account

- Personalise account names – they even appear on your statements so that you'll recognise them
- Transfer money to and from your Savings account

All this added convenience doesn't compromise your security. We have a fiendish security protection system to safeguard your account. We also back it up with our Online Banking guarantee. This states that in the unlikely event that you innocently suffer internet fraud on your Barclays Current or Savings account(s), we guarantee to cover the loss – no matter how much is taken from your account[†]. All you pay is the cost of a local call while you're online.*

If you haven't already applied for Online Banking you won't be surprised to hear that you can apply online at www.ibank.barclays.co.uk or via a phone line by calling 0845 600 23 23** any time from 7am until 11pm, Monday to Sunday. How's that for convenience?

And if you have already registered – the paperwork is on its way to you. If you haven't received your membership details within six days of applying, please give us a call on 0845 7 555 555** or let your Personal Banker know.

**Online banking availability excludes scheduled maintenance or inaccessibility due to factors/events outside our control.
†Terms and conditions apply. For full details see our website at www.barclays.co.uk/onlineguarantee.
**Calls to 0845 numbers will cost no more than 4p per minute, minimum call charge 5.5p (current at September 2006) for BT customers. The price on non-BT phone line may be different. Calls may be monitored for training and security purposes.

(Source: Barclays Bank, 2006)

# Text 5.4

## Ideas for starting your own business

Another helpful guide is *101 Ways to Start Your Own Business* (Christine Ingham, 1998, Kogan Page). The 1998 edition is fully revised and provides you with 101 interesting and original ideas for setting up on your own. As well as giving an overview of each idea, Christine Ingham says what sort of person the idea would appeal to; gives the advantages and disadvantages; and future possibilities of the idea. Where possible, the book lists useful addresses and publications.

Accommodation
Antiques
Architectural salvage
Bicycle repairs
Bodyguard service
Book search service
Box designs
Business support service
Buying and renovating properties
Buying an existing business
Cake design
Calligraphy
Car care
Card-mailing service
Careers adviser
Catering service
Children's party entertainer
Cleaning antiques
Community business
Companions agency
Complementary therapies
Contract cleaning
Counselling
Courier services
Craft work
Cultivating new plants
Dealing in art
Driving tuition
Film making
Florist's commission work
Fortune telling
Franchising
Fund raising
Garden work

Gift-buying service
Grave care
Greeting card design
Hairdressing
History of houses
House name and number plates
Image consultant
Importing
Indexing
Internet businesses
Introducing sidelines
Inventions
Ironing service
Letting properties service
Local walks and tours
Magazine publishing
Mail order
Making kits
Management consultancy
Market stalls
Mini-cab services
Multimedia design
Natural toiletry products
Nursing home
Office equipment cleaning
Office lunches
Organic food supplier
Organising conferences
Party DJ
Party planning
Personal trainer
Personalised gifts
Pet food supplier
Pet sitting and walking

Picture library
Premium rate telephone lines
Print selling
Private investigation agency
Product agent
Professional's manager or agent
Property-finding service
Property maintenance
Publishers' remainders
Reconditioning equipment
Recording studio
Renovating junk furniture
Reupholstering
Running a play group
Secondhand goods
Security work
Sell your knowledge
Speciality foods
Surplus stock
Telecottages
Teleworking
Themed cafés
Toy making
Tracing family trees
Training for businesses
Translation work
Tuition
Voluntary group
Wedding consultant
Window boxes
Window cleaning
Window dressing
Writing

(Source: www.homeworking.com/library/basic.htm, 2007)

# Extract 5.5

## Mobile devices

In the first quarter 2007, the total mobile device volume achieved by our Mobile Phones, Multimedia and Enterprise Solutions business groups reached 91.1 million units, representing 21% year-on-year growth and a 14% sequential decrease. The overall industry volume for the same period reached an estimated 253 million units, representing 18% year-on-year growth and a 13% sequential decrease.

Converged device industry volumes increased to an estimated 23.5 million units, compared with an estimated 17 million units in the first quarter 2006. Nokia's own converged device volumes rose to 11.8 million units, compared with 8.5 million units in the first quarter 2006. Nokia shipped close to eight million Nokia Nseries and more than one million Nokia Eseries devices during the first quarter 2007.

The following chart sets out Nokia's mobile device volumes for the periods indicated, as well as the year-on-year and sequential growth rates by geographic area.

**Nokia mobile device volume by geographic area**

| (million units) | Q1 2007 | Q1 2006 | YoY change (%) | | Q4 2006 | QoQ change (%) |
|---|---|---|---|---|---|---|
| Europe | 23.9 | 20.4 | 17.7 | 33.3 | | −28.3 |
| Middle East and Africa | 15.7 | 11.9 | 31.8 | 15.5 | | 1.3 |
| China | 15.7 | 10.9 | 43.4 | 14.6 | | 7.8 |
| Asia-Pacific | 23.7 | 16.4 | 44.7 | 23.7 | | 0.3 |
| North America | 4.8 | 8.4 | −42.5 | 5.9 | | −19.0 |
| Latin America | 7.3 | 7.1 | 2.4 | 12.5 | | −41.8 |
| Total | 91.1 | 75.1 | 21.4 | 105.5 | | −13.7 |

Based on our preliminary market estimate, Nokia's market share for the first quarter 2007 was 36%, compared with 35% in the first quarter 2006 and 36% in the fourth quarter 2006. Nokia's year-on-year market share increase was driven primarily by strong gains in Asia-Pacific and Europe that more than offset a significant market share decline in North America. Year-on-year market share was approximately at the same level in China, Latin America and Middle East and Africa. Sequentially, Nokia's market share was approximately at the same level as in fourth quarter 2006, globally as well as in each geographic area. The sequential decline in first quarter industry volumes was similar to previous years, however we believe there has been an impact in the market from the excess inventory of certain of our competitors' products.

Nokia's average selling price in the first quarter 2007 was EUR 89, down from EUR 103 in the first quarter 2006 and at the same level as in the fourth quarter 2006. The lower year-on-year ASP in the first quarter 2007 was primarily the result of a significantly higher proportion of entry-level device sales, where the industry growth especially in the emerging markets has been strong and where

Nokia's share has been growing. In addition, certain ageing higher end products in our portfolio were viewed as less competitive in various markets. Sequentially, first quarter 2007 ASPs were impacted by a higher percentage of entry-level device sales. That sequential development was offset by strong sales of our higher ASP devices, particularly from the Multimedia business group.

## Business groups

**Mobile Phones:** first quarter 2007 net sales decreased 5% to EUR 5.6 billion, compared with EUR 5.9 billion in the first quarter 2006. Strong overall volume growth was not enough to offset a significant ASP decline year on year, driven primarily by a higher proportion of entry-level sales. Net sales decreased in all regions except Asia-Pacific. Net sales were down significantly in North America and to a lesser degree in Latin America, Middle East and Africa, Europe and China.

Mobile Phones reported operating profit in the first quarter 2007 decreased 14% to EUR 936 million, compared with EUR 1.1 billion in the first quarter 2006, with an operating margin of 16.8% (18.5%). Reported first quarter 2007 operating profit included total charges of EUR 35 million, of which EUR 25 million was related to the restructuring of a subsidiary company and EUR 10 million was mainly related to restructuring in Customer and Market Operations. First quarter 2006 reported operating profit included a EUR 14 million initial restructuring charge for the CDMA business. [CDMA stands for Code Division Multiple Access, which is a transmission technique used by various digital communication technologies, e.g. by mobile phones.] Operating profit for the first quarter 2007 excluding the charges was EUR 971 million, with an operating margin of 17.4% (18.7%). The decrease in operating profit for the first quarter 2007, excluding the special items, was primarily caused by lower sales of higher end, higher margin devices, and an increase in sales and marketing expenses, compared to the first quarter 2006.

(Source: http://www.nokia.com/A4132057)

# Session 6 resources

## Text 6.1

### An extract from a workplace proposal

The training organisation which provides technical training for managers in our company has recently reported that attendance at training sessions is consistently poor in this department compared with other departments. Similar absenteeism has been reported from other seminars and workshops. Such absenteeism disrupts the progress of the courses, puts our department in a bad light, and ultimately wastes the company's money.

Our goal is to provide training of relevance to our employees and their work and to ensure that they get the maximum benefit from participation. If managers are not attending the courses that they have volunteered for, there is clearly something wrong. In order to address this, we first need to know what the true level of attendance is and what factors contribute to non-attendance. We therefore propose a rapid investigation into attendance at all the training programmes and events that we organise for our staff.

Under the direction of the Management Team, the investigation should involve three phases of information collection. The first phase is to collect detailed attendance registers from the supplier organisations in order to analyse whether absenteeism relates to particular employees or particular programmes – or whether it is a more widespread phenomenon. Secondly, team managers should hold brief interviews with course participants to determine why they miss sessions and how they feel about the programmes offered. Finally, senior managers should hold brief interviews with team managers in order to discuss whether there are workload, motivational or control problems that lead to non-attendance. The results of these three forms of enquiry should be passed to the training manager before the end of the month. She should report to next month's Management Team meeting, where, with complete information at their disposal, they can consider ways to improve attendance.

We are convinced that the proposed action will provide the department with the necessary information on which to base further action to remedy the problem of absenteeism from training programmes. We recommend it to the Management Team for approval.

(Source: written for the course by David Lewis, external consultant)

# Text 6.2

# A PROPOSAL FOR THE REORGANIZATION OF DEPARTMENT X OF THE STORE

## PREFACE

This is a proposal for the reorganization of Department X, Draperies and Bed-coverings, a subdivision of the Linens Department of The Store. It is being presented to the Chairman and Chief Executive Officer of the corporation.

The conclusions and recommendations are based upon my personal experience as a Sales Associate who has worked in the Linens Department of both the Birmingham and Plymouth stores, and upon observations I made while visiting three other stores – Sheffield, Coventry and Liverpool. In the Birmingham store I worked primarily in Department X, while in the Plymouth store I have' worked across the entire Linens Department.

The purpose of this proposal is to draw attention to the unique potential of Department X and to show how it could be developed to become a more productive department. These recommendations can either be implemented as they stand (for example, the recommendation for the preparation of a procedure manual), or they can be used as starting points for further investigation (for example, the recommendation for a complete change in departmental structure).

## INTRODUCTION

Although The Store offers its customers a complete custom service for draperies, upholstery, and blinds – the Shop-at-Home Department – many customers prefer to take advantage of the less costly, 'do-it-yourself' alternative that Department X provides: made-to-measure and special-order draperies and bedcoverings.

Because this is especially true in today's economy, the unique offerings of Department X contain a very high sales potential for The Store. The problem, however, is that incomplete training of the Sales Associates assigned to that department and the lack of clearly defined operating procedure leads to loss of sales, dissatisfied customers, and withdrawal of patronage.

It is the purpose of this proposal to recommend those changes that seem most likely to rectify this problem and to help develop the sales potential of this department. These recommendations cover the following areas:

- training of Sales Associates and the development of a professional staff,
- preparation of a procedure manual to be used both as a training and a reference tool,
- and changes in the physical layout of the department and to its internal structure.

[...]

Inadequate training and lack of clearly defined procedures are the department's greatest deficiencies and these in turn result in a frustrated selling staff who are not being motivated to produce. By implementing the changes proposed, The Store could make a real start in turning the department around and seeing that it develops its large and very special sales potential.

## BASIS FOR RECOMMENDATIONS

[...]

## RECOMMENDATIONS

### *Procedure Manual*

[...]

### *Training of Sales Associates*

Ranking in equal importance with the preparation of a comprehensive procedure manual in the reorganization of Department X is the training of the Sales Associates who will work in this area. Besides the general training all Sales Associates receive in selling, policy, and procedures, those Associates assigned to Department X should receive specialized training.

#### *Sales Techniques*

Very often a customer who wants to order blinds or draperies has only a vague notion of what is involved. The first thing they need is accurate and precise answers to their questions which will include how to take measurements, what kinds of fabrics and linings should be used, and what kinds of hardware are available.

While all this information will be in the procedure manual under Product Information, the Sales Associate must be ready to anticipate questions not asked and must not be reluctant to ask additional questions such as type of room, amount of sunlight, and colour scheme in order to ascertain what it is that the customer wants to achieve. It is by becoming actively involved with the customer and what they want that the best sales are made and long-lasting customer relations built.

It is on this type of selling technique that the specialized training for Department X Sales Associates should focus. It is not enough to know the products, although that knowledge is imperative, but the Sales Associate must be ready to spend time with the customer, listening to them and satisfying their needs. Compared [with] other sales made in the Linens Department, much more time per customer will be spent in Department X, but it should be remembered that individual sales in that department are usually much higher than most individual sales in the rest of the Linens Department and that the time spent is well justified.

#### *Procedure Manual*

The first step in training the Sales Associate for Department X is complete familiarization with the procedure manual. This will give them a comprehensive overview of the department and its products, and will also give them access to the department's primary reference tool. If the Associate is well trained in the use of the manual, they will be able to find the answers to almost all of their and their customer's questions.

*Meetings with Buyer and Vendors*
Another aspect of the training should be direct contact with both the Department X buyer and with the various vendors (manufacturers) whose products are sold in the department.Through meeting with the buyer, the Sales Associate will learn about departmental goals and sales philosophy. Such information will enable the Associate to direct their selling efforts toward these ends.

Meeting with the various vendors will increase the Sales Associate's knowledge of the product and will build personal rapport between the Associate and the vendor's representative which could prove invaluable in the solution of problems. Such open lines of communication would also prove valuable when there are changes of procedures or products at the vendor's.

However, the most important aspect of the training of the Sales Associates working in Department X is that discussed in the first few paragraphs of this section. The Associate must be willing to spend time with the customer, answering, asking, and anticipating questions – in short, being responsive to their needs.

## Physical Layout of Department

[...]

## Departmental Structure

Presently, Department X is part of the Linens Department and the foregoing recommendations have focused on changes in procedures and displays within the department as it exists now. However, this final recommendation for the reorganization of Department X concerns a complete restructuring of the department. In fact, if a thorough reorganization of Department X is to be accomplished, this restructuring should really be the first step.

*Separate Department*
Restructuring the department would include, first of all, the actual separation of Department X from the Linens Department, creating a new department altogether (Draperies and Bedcoverings), with its own manager and a sales staff that is *not* interchangeable with the Linens Department. This is recommended because the unique offerings of Department X are being lost by its submersion in the Linens Department, and its full sales potential is not being realized.

*Regular Staff*
Secondly, in conjunction with the specialized training of Sales Associates previously discussed, emphasis should be placed on the development of a regular staff of Sales Associates, both full- and part-time, for the new department. Such a staff would be more expert than that being used now, not having to work in a department whose products are as diverse as those of the present Linens Department,

and this increased expertise would mean greater ability to provide the customer with what [they] want or to suggest workable alternatives to meet [their] needs. Department X could then begin to provide a very real alternative to customizing and ready-mades.

*Remuneration*

One of the key factors in the development of such a professional sales staff is motivation. If the right incentives are used to motivate the sales staff, that and their greater expertise in the products and services they are selling would significantly increase the sales volume of the department.

Because the best incentive in a sales position is the money that can be earned, it is recommended that the regular staff of the new department be paid on a part-commission basis. A schedule that paid the Sales Associate 10% of their gross sales in excess of their base salary would certainly prove to be an effective incentive and greatly facilitate the recruitment and retention of a regular and highly professional sales staff.

## CONCLUSION

In today's economy, the consumer is trying to get as much for their money as possible while spending as little of it as possible. Because of this more conservative attitude toward spending, the consumer is shopping more carefully and considering their purchases more thoughtfully.

This new attitude can be used to develop the sales potential of Department X, which offers a very real alternative to the expense of custom-made merchandise and the limitations of ready-made. However, this potential cannot be realized by a department that is poorly organized and staffed by inadequately trained personnel.

It has been the purpose of this proposal to make certain recommendations for the reorganization of Department X which could result in an efficiently structured department, staffed by a core of professional, competent, and knowledgeable Sales Associates. This newly organized department would be able to offer consumers a large selection of reasonably priced decorating products of good quality, while its sales staff would be able to answer questions and provide the product information needed to buy wisely. Department X could then begin to realize its full sales potential and make an increased contribution to The Store's overall sales volume.

(Source: adapted from Neufeld, J., 1987, *A Handbook for Technical Communication*, London, Prentice-Hall International, pp. 174–81)

# Text 6.3

## Attendance management

Tesco, the retailer and largest private sector employer in the UK, achieved a one-fifth reduction of absence levels (to 4.6%) in one year after introducing 'attendance management procedures'. One HR manager said, 'Operating in an incredibly tight market forces us to control costs wherever we can. Absenteeism was costing us between £30 million and £40 million a year and was impacting on customer service'. Every Tesco employee who takes sick leave of any duration now has to have a 'return to work interview' with one of the store managers.

In a substantial number of cases, it has emerged that the employee was off for domestic or family reasons – looking after a sick child for example. If this is the case, the employee is given various options. The absence can be taken as holiday, as unpaid leave or set off against overtime. People who then have two periods of sickness within 24 weeks are then drawn into the 'attendance management' process where their attendance is monitored. If they then have a third absence, or if their total time off sick goes above 5%, they are interviewed again and banned from doing overtime for 6 weeks. In the interview they will be asked more about their time off – whether there are common patterns to the different periods of illness. Occupational health services will be made available if a pattern is established; for example if they are suffering from repeated back trouble or they want to space their shifts out differently. If over the next 12 weeks their sickness record does not improve they will get another interview and probably a verbal warning. If within the next 8 weeks there is no improvement they could get a final written warning and possibly be sacked. Tesco says it has tried to be open and fair with staff. An employee will not have to go through this process if there is a clear medical problem.

(Source: MacErlean, N., 2000, 'Pulling the rug under the "sickie"', *The Observer*, 20 August)

# Acknowledgements

Grateful acknowledgement is made to the following sources:

## Text

Page 8, Text 1.4: Adapted from Doherty, M. et al., 1987, *Write for Business*, Harlow, Pearson Longman, pp. 6–7; page 68, extract 5.5: Nokia Q12007, www.nokia.com; pages 71–74, Text 6.2: Neufeld, J.K. (1987) Excerpts pp. 174, 175, 178, 179, 180 and 181 from *A Handbook for Technical Writing*; © 1987 by Prentice-Hall, Inc. Reprinted by permission of Pearson Education, Inc. Users may not print out or reproduce copies of the material without permission of Pearson Education, Inc.; page 75, Text 6.3: MacErlean, N. (2000) Observer Business Pages, 'Pulling the rug under the "sickie": Absenteeism is a pnational disease. Neasa MacErlean looks at employers' drastic remedies'; August 20, 2000, Guardian Newspapers Limited.

## Tables

Pages 8–9, Text 1.5: Adapted from Manalo, E. et al., 2006, *The Business of Writing*, London, Pearson, p. 23; page 21, Text 1.13: Adapted from Brieger, N and Comfort, J., 1992, *Language Reference for Business English*, London, Prentice-Hall, p 25; page 67, Text 5.4: www.homeworking.com; page 68: Nokia Q12007, www.nokia.com.

## Figures

Page 11, Figures 1 and 2, page 25, Figure 2, page 29, Figure 2: Porter, M.E. (1980) *Competitive Strategy*, The Free Press, New York; page 40, Figure 3.1: Arnold, J., Cooper, C.L. and Robertson, I.T. (1995) *Work Psychology: Understanding Human Behaviour in the Workplace* (2nd edn), Pitman, p. 395, Figure 19.1; page 46, Figure 2: Armson, R., Martin, J., Carr, S., Spear, R. and Walsh, A. (1995) 'Culture and management', *Managing in Organisations*, Milton Keynes, The Open University; page 46, Figure 3: Coates, D. (2000) Chapter 3 in M. Lucas (ed.) *Understanding Business: Environments* (B200 Reader 1), London, Routledge; page 64, Text 5.1: NatWest Travel Service (2007) 'Tantalising offers to whet your appetite, 31 October 2007, Royal Bank of Scotland; page 65, Text 5.2, page 66, Text 5.3: © Barclays Bank.